Also by Sigurd F. Olson

The Singing Wilderness (1956)
Listening Point (1958)
The Lonely Land (1961)
Runes of the North (1963)
Open Horizons (1969)
Reflections From the North
Country (1976)
Of Time and Place (1982)

These are Borzoi Books published
in New York by Alfred A. Knopf

Sigurd F.
Olson's
Wilderness
Days

Alfred A. Knopf
New York, 1984

Sigurd F. Olson's Wilderness Days

This is a Borzoi Book published by Alfred A. Knopf, Inc.

Copyright © 1956, 1958, 1961, 1963, 1969, 1972 by Sigurd F. Olson
All rights reserved under International and Pan-American Copyright Conven-
tions. Published in the United States by Alfred A. Knopf, Inc., New York, and
simultaneously in Canada by Random House of Canada Limited, Toronto. Dis-
tributed by Random House, Inc., New York.

Library of Congress Cataloging in Publication Data:
Olson, Sigurd F. Sigurd F. Olson's Wilderness Days.
1. Natural history — Outdoor books. 2. Nature. 3. Outdoor life.
I. Title: Wilderness Days.
QH81.O67   1972   500.9'08   72-2243
ISBN 0-394-47155-5
ISBN 0-394-48312-X (special ed.)

Manufactured in the United States of America
First Edition

Published September 7, 1972
Reprinted Five Times
Seventh Printing, January 1984

*To all who have listened to
the Pipes of Pan
along the waterways of
the north*

Acknowledgments

My sincere appreciation goes to Marie Rodell, my agent, to Angus Cameron, my editor, and to the entire staff of Alfred A. Knopf, Inc., for suggestions in the planning and final preparation of the book. Special thanks are due my wife, Elizabeth, for encouragement and criticism, and to Ann Langen for the careful editing, typing, and intricate manipulations involved in weaving together the manuscript.

The use of some of the many black-and-white sketches of Francis Lee Jaques, Robert Hines, and Leslie Kouba added much to the format, and to them I am again indebted. I am grateful to Dr. J. Arnold Bolz for a selection of superb color transparencies that added new life, beauty, and meaning to *Wilderness Days*.

Contents

Four Seasons of Photographs
by J. Arnold Bolz

Spring

First Page:

Marsh marigolds. Loon Lake, St. Louis County, Minnesota.

Second Page: (left to right, top to bottom)

A spring torrent. Loon Falls, St. Louis County, Minnesota.

Frozen spray and orange lichens on palisade. North shore, Lake Superior, Cook County, Minnesota.

A clearing evening storm. Crooked Lake, St. Louis County, Minnesota.

Moss-covered rock at water's edge. Saganaga Lake, Cook County, Minnesota.

The pounding rush of water. Upper gorge, Vermilion River, St. Louis County, Minnesota.

The misty mood of morning. Lac la Croix, St. Louis County, Minnesota.

Third Page: (left to right, top to bottom)

The silence of early morning. Sand Point Lake, St. Louis County, Minnesota.

A budding birch on a cliff. Lac la Croix, St. Louis County, Minnesota.

Still morning waters. Saganaga Lake, Cook County, Minnesota.

In a spruce and tamarack bog: laurel, Labrador tea, and cotton grass. Echo Trail, St. Louis County, Minnesota.

Moss soaked in ground-water run-off. Lac la Croix, St. Louis County, Minnesota.

Buttercups. Lilac Lake, Ontario, Canada.

Fourth Page:

Young doe browsing. Echo River, St. Louis County, Minnesota.

Summer

First Page:

Linnaea and dwarf dogwood. Gunflint Trail, Cook County, Minnesota.

Second Page: (left to right, top to bottom)

Blueberries. Lac la Croix, St. Louis County, Minnesota.

Evening storm after a hot summer day. Gunflint Trail, Cook County, Minnesota.

Indian pictographs. Darkey Lake, Ontario, Canada.

Lake bottom through clear green water. Argo Lake, Ontario, Canada.

An old windfall. Lac la Croix, St. Louis County, Minnesota.

Rock intrusions. Kawnipi Falls chain, Ontario, Canada.

Third Page: (*left to right, top to bottom*)
Harebells and lichens on a vertical cliff. Namakan Lake, Ontario, Canada.
Moss-grown cedars. Rebecca Falls, Ontario, Canada.
Brink of Curtain Falls. Crooked Lake, St. Louis County, Minnesota.
Virgin Norway pine. Lady Boot Bay, Lac la Croix, St. Louis County, Minnesota.
Sun through early morning mist. Budside Lake, Ontario, Canada.
Caribou moss. Lac la Croix, St. Louis County, Minnesota.
Fourth Page:
Moss bank under jackpines. Knife Lake, Lake County, Minnesota.

#

First Page:
An eddy of foam and leaves. Little Indian Sioux River, St. Louis County, Minnesota.
Second Page: (*left to right, top to bottom*)
Autumn reflections. Little Indian Sioux River, St. Louis County, Minnesota.
Aspen and maple. Echo Trail, St. Louis County, Minnesota.
Smoky gold: tamaracks. Swamp Lake, Lake County, Minnesota.
Early October shoreline. Namakan Lake, St. Louis County, Minnesota.
Late-afternoon reflections. Echo River, St. Louis County, Minnesota.
Horizons of Lake Kahshapiwi. Ontario, Canada.
Third Page: (*left to right, top to bottom*)
The silhouette of grasses at sunset. Bottle Lake, St. Louis County, Minnesota.
Needles and leaves. Birch Lake, Ontario, Canada.
Morning fog and a rising sun. Lac la Croix, Ontario, Canada.
Scrub oak. Crane Lake, St. Louis County, Minnesota.
First coating of ice and frost. Gunflint Trail, Lake County, Minnesota.
Norway pine and maples. Gunflint Trail, Lake County, Minnesota.
Fourth Page:
Early frost on grasses and raspberry leaves. Fernberg Trail, St. Louis County, Minnesota.

#

First Page:
A soft and quiet midwinter snow. Gunflint Trail, Cook County, Minnesota.
Second Page: (*left to right, top to bottom*)
Lower gorge of the Vermilion River. St. Louis County, Minnesota.
February sunrise. Namakan River, Ontario, Canada.
Frost-plumed grass on a cliff. Second Lake, St. Louis County, Minnesota.

Islands of Lac la Croix. St. Louis County, Minnesota.
Wind sculpture. Little Vermilion Lake, St. Louis County, Minnesota.
50° below zero. Kawishiwi River, St. Louis County, Minnesota.
Third Page: (left to right, top to bottom)
Long shadows of late afternoon. Iron Lake, Cook County, Minnesota.
Icebound islands. Namakan Lake, St. Louis County, Minnesota.
Iced pebbles. North shore, Lake Superior, Cook County, Minnesota.
Winter filigree. Gunflint Trail, Cook County, Minnesota.
The December sun sets early. Lac la Croix, St. Louis County, Minnesota.
Winter flowage: First Lake Creek. St. Louis County, Minnesota.
Fourth Page:
Frozen spray on birch and rock. Lake Superior, Cook County, Minnesota.

Author's Note

My first book, *The Singing Wilderness*, was an attempt to catch the true meaning of primitive experience in the wilderness canoe country of the Quetico-Superior. *Listening Point*, in which I described the building of my cabin and what it meant to me after many years of a *voyageur*'s life, was the realization of the truth that from any specific point you can see all of the north. *The Lonely Land*, an account of an expedition down that once famous route of trade and exploration known as the Churchill River, was written to recapture the challenges and rewards of all distant waterways. *Runes of the North* was a search for further meaning, following in the footsteps of the Finnish bards who gave us the great runic poem *Kalevala*. *Open Horizons* was a somewhat autobiographical tale of the unknown horizons that have influenced my life.

The reactions of readers over the years have been gratifying, and many have written about my books, telling of the chapters that had special meaning for them. Some liked the adventures of fighting storms, running rapids, or finding their way through unmapped terrain; others, the subtler feelings and moods of the country; many, the sense of coming to feel at home far from civilization, an identification with the land that goes deep down into the primal well of awareness that is the story of all mankind.

As time passed, a pattern began to emerge, for many had chosen the same chapters or had almost identical reactions to what I had written. I began exploring then the idea of selecting those parts mentioned most frequently, crystallizing perhaps in one volume not only the essence of the regions described or the experiences I had had, but also the feelings of those who had actually shared these adventures with me or who possibly were only *voyageurs* at heart.

Because it seemed logical to follow the seasons in such a book, I used the old format of *The Singing Wilderness*, knowing that anyone who has traveled the wilds or even dreamed about them invariably thinks of the natural progression of the seasons in order to achieve a sense of continuity.

The book became *Wilderness Days*, for each of the chapters chosen was exactly that, a vignette of experience or a highlight many have known. I chose them primarily for those who have written to me, but some for myself, knowing that even though they were not included in the list compiled, there was in them the same sense of rapport and empathy that brought the book into being.

Prologue: My Wilderness World

My wilderness world has to do with the calling of loons, northern lights, and the great silences of a land lying north and northwest of Lake Superior. It is concerned with the simple joys, timelessness, and perspective found in a way of life close to the past. I have heard the song of this wilderness from the border country of Minnesota and Ontario to the lonely reaches of the tundra close to the Arctic, but I hear it best in the beautiful lake region of the Quetico-Superior, where travel is still by pack and canoe over the ancient trails of Indians and *voyageurs.*

I have listened to it on misty migration nights when the dark has been alive with the high calling of birds, in rapids when the air was full of their rushing thunder, at dawn with the mists moving out of the bays, and on cold winter nights when the stars seemed close enough to touch. The music can be heard in the soft guttering of an open fire or in the beat of rain on a tent, and sometimes long afterward, like an echo out of the past, you know it is there in some quiet place, or while doing a simple task out of doors.

I have discovered I am not alone in my listening. Everyone is listening for something, and the search for places where the singing may be heard goes on everywhere. It is part of the hunger all of us have for a time when we were closer to lakes and rivers, to mountains, meadows, and forests than we are today. Because of our almost forgotten past there is a restlessness within us, an impatience, which modern life with its comforts and distractions does not satisfy. We sense intuitively there must be something more, search for panaceas to give us a sense of reality, and fill our days and nights with such activity and busyness there is little time to think. When the pace stops we are often lost, and plunge once more into the maelstrom, hoping if we move fast enough we may somehow fill the void within us. We may not know exactly what we are listening for, but we hunt as instinctively as sick animals look for healing herbs.

The search is rewarding, for somehow in the process we tap deep wells of racial experience which give us a feeling of being part of an existence where life was simple and satisfactions real. Uncounted centuries of the primitive have left their mark upon us, and civilization has not changed emotional needs which were ours before the dawn of history. This is the reason for the hunger, the listening and constant search. Should we actually glimpse the ancient glory or hear the song of the wilderness, cities with their confusion become quiet, speed and turmoil are slowed to the pace of the seasons, and tensions are replaced with calm.

I vividly remember the first time I heard the haunting music. It was on the shore of Lake Michigan at the end of a broken pier where a translucent pool shone among the rocks. Seagulls wheeled and cried above me. Waves crashed against the pier and I was alone in a wild and lovely place, part of the wind and water and all the sounds, colors, and feelings of the natural world I had found. That day I entered into a life of indescribable beauty and delight.

Years later I heard the song again in a virgin forest of tremendous trees. Those ancient black boles, green-gold twilight filtering through the high, moaning tops — the moss-cushioned silence still echoes in my mind.

Another time, at the headwaters of a little creek I found a spring pool surrounded by great trees, yellow birch, white pine, and hemlock. I lay on a shelf of lichen-covered rock above it, looking down into the deep clear water. A school of brook trout lay near the bottom, fanning their fins as they faced the flow from above. When I tossed a cone onto the surface they rose as one and the pool came alive with their splashing. Then I heard the singing clearly, for here was a bit of primitive America, untouched and unseen.

Such places of my boyhood seemed the answer to all my needs, and their magic and wonder belonged to me alone. My perceptions were uncluttered, my childish impressions pure and uninfluenced, my feelings true, and in them I know now was the ancient realization of oneness so hard to recognize as life becomes more involved.

John Masefield, in speaking of his own first contacts with what he called the greater life, said: "I believe that life to be the source of all that is of glory and goodness in this world and modern man, not knowing that, is dwelling in death."

Those first experiences were the forerunners of many others that gave me a desire ultimately leading me into the far wilderness regions of the continent in the hope I might find them again. Since those early days I have known the mountains of the east and west, cypress swamps and savannas of the south, colorful deserts and ranges of the southwest, the limitless expanses of the Canadian Shield, the muskegs and tundras of the far north. There has always been the sense of expectancy, the search and the listening, and I have found that when I have renewed in even the slightest way the primal sense of belonging I knew as a child, whenever I have glimpsed, if only for an instant, the glory I knew then, my spirits soared.

It made no difference where I happened to be — on the Mackenzie, Churchill, the shores of Hudson Bay, in the Athabasca country, on the Great Slave or Great Bear, in the Yukon or Alaska following the routes of *voyageurs* and early explorers — the real purpose was still the search which began in the Quetico-Superior. This vast and lonely land was still wilderness and I knew the awe and challenge of the first explorers. I felt the great silences there, the heightened awareness that comes from a certain amount of danger, and the calm and timelessness which balanced the tensions of the world I had left.

In this wilderness I saw more clearly those values and influences which have molded the human race over the long centuries. I knew, too, there are moments of insight when ancient truths stand out more vividly and one senses again his relationship to the earth and all life. Such times are worth waiting for, and when they come in some unheralded instant of knowing are of the purest gold.

"Man," as Emerson once said, "is a dwarf of himself and so ancient beliefs and feelings are in a sense vestigial remains of the common origins of man's inner world." This inner world has to do with the past from which we came, with cosmic rhythms and the deep feelings men have for an unchanged environment. It is a communion with the natural world, a basic awareness of earth wisdom which, since the beginning of man's rise from the primitive, has nourished his visions and dreams.

Such things belong to the shadowy realm of the intangibles, more real and significant, perhaps, than can be seen, for they give rise to achievements of the spirit and to all cultural advance.

During the years of roaming the far north I discovered the meaning of open horizons, for on those great waters sometimes islands and headlands disappeared in the distance and waters merged with the sky in a mirage of hazy blue. Hours and often days later, when the islands appeared again and shores became real, it seemed as though I had passed through a door into the beyond itself. On those expeditions there was time to think during long hours of uninterrupted paddling, and I knew that life is a series of open horizons with one no sooner completed than another looms ahead. Some are traversed swiftly while others extend so far into the distance one cannot predict their end. Penetrations into the unknown all give meaning to what has gone before and courage for what is to come. More than physical features, they become horizons of mind and spirit, and when one looks backward he finds they have blended into the panorama of his life.

Open horizons of childhood show the dawning awareness of beauty at a time when the Pipes of Pan can still be heard; those of youth retrace the ages of mythology, the long millennia of the hunter and freedom of the wilderness. The open horizons of young manhood bring broader concepts, the impact of knowledge, reverence for the living world, relationships to others and to the earth itself; those of maturity show concern for the living place of man, perspective on his long journey from the primitive, and understanding of the great imponderables.

What a man finally becomes, how he adjusts to his world is a composite of all the horizons he has explored. They have marked him, left indelible imprints on attitudes and convictions, and given his life direction and meaning. What one remembers of any wilderness travel are not the details of rapids, camps, or miles covered, but a broad montage of major headlands passed and the sweep of the land.

No two *voyageurs* enter open horizons in the same way, but all have in common a certain evolution of vision and perspective. Each knows when there are no beckoning mirages ahead a man dies, but with an open horizon constantly before him, life can be an eternal challenge.

I learned that nothing stands alone, no matter how insignificant it might seem. Within a vein of rose quartz in a granite ledge could be read the geological history of the planet; from an old stump of a tree, the ecological succession of the entire plant kingdom; from an Indian legend, the dreams of all mankind. No longer would it be necessary to travel thousands of miles, no longer the unending search for the essence of wilderness and the singing, no longer the need for new open horizons. All these I could remember from any point I chose. With the knowledge acquired and the sense of intimacy with all living things and the earth itself, I could explore the entire north and all its life — including my own.

After years of searching I found a place of my own and called it Listening Point, because only when one comes to listen, only when one is aware and still, can things be seen and heard. It would speak to me of silence and solitude, of belonging and wonder and beauty. Though only a glaciated spit of rock on an island-dotted lake with twisted pines and caribou moss, I knew it would grow into my life and the lives of all who shared it with me. However small a part of the vastness reaching far to the Arctic, from it I could survey the whole, hear the singing of the wilderness, and catch perhaps the music of the spheres.

I know now this concept is one of the greatest satisfactions of man, that when he gazed upon the earth and sky with wonder, sensed the first vague glimmerings of meaning in the universe, the world of knowledge and spirit was opened to him. I also believe that, while such inherent joys are often lost, deep within us their latent glow can be fanned to flame again by awareness and an open mind. Anyone can have a Listening Point. It does not have to be in the north or the wilderness, simply some place of quiet where the natural world still lives and one can look into the cosmic distances of space and hear the eternal music to which man has always listened.

Spring

Spring in the north begins while the land
is still frozen and white. It comes with
the winds and gales and drifting snows
toward mid-March in a barely perceptible
hint of warmth as the sun climbs high.
As days lengthen there are smells of
balsam and pine and warming earth on
southern slopes. And if one listens, there
are telltale sounds as well: the crystalline
tinkling of melting ice and snow, the soft
chuckling of running water in creeks and in
millions of rivulets breaking free.
Toward April there are new bird songs,
the keening of killdeer in low places, the
mating whistle of chickadees in the balsams,
the mewing of seagulls along open leads
of water on the lakes. And there are colors
too: a rosy-purplish blush in the tops of
birches, dogwood stems red against the
white.
As snowbanks sink and then disappear,
there are drifts of pussy willows in still
frozen swamps and then, almost overnight,
a brush of Nile green on aspen-covered
ridges and in warm cozy nooks out of the
wind the rosy hue of maples bursting
into bloom. Though the forest floor is still
brown and the smell of it is of mold and
wetness, by mid-May it is gay with blue
and white hepatica, pink anemones, and—
along the flooded banks of creeks—marsh
marigolds.
All life is stirring now in lakes, and ponds,
and streams, and in myriad tiny pools of
snow water. The earth is awake at last after
the long winter's sleep, and within it is a
quickening. After half a year of frozen silence,
spring is a miracle of rebirth, a time of
rare transcendent beauty and promise.

The Winds of March

To anyone who has spent a winter in the north and known the depths to which the snow can reach, known the weeks when the mercury stays below zero, the first hint of spring is a major event. You must live in the north to understand it. You cannot just come up for it as you might go to Florida for the sunshine and the surf. To appreciate it, you must wait for it a long time, hope and dream about it, and go through considerable enduring.

Looking forward to spring plays the same part in morale building in the north as rumors do in an army camp. The very thought of it is something to live for when the days are bitter and winter is stretching out a little longer than it should. When March comes in, no matter how cold and blustery it is, the time is ripe for signs.

It makes no difference if the ice is still thick on the lakes and the drifts are as deep as ever. When that something is in the wind, the entire situation is changed. I caught it one day toward the end of March, just the faintest hint of softness in the air, a slight tempering of the cold, a promise that hadn't been there before. I forgot my work and all immediate responsibilities and went out of doors. On the sunny side of the house I stood and looked and waited, expecting something to happen, but the drifts were the same and the wind out of the northwest was not different from the gales that had piled the snows for the past months. Then I became conscious of the sound of trickling water beside me—nothing more than a whisper, but the forerunner, I knew, of a million coming trickles that would take down the drifts of the entire countryside.

It was there that I got my first real whiff of spring: the smell of warming trees, pines and balsams and resins beginning to soften on the south slopes. I waited there and sniffed like a hound on the loose, winnowing through my starved nostrils the whole composite picture of coming events.

Below the house was a little patch of bare ground with a big drift curling over it. There the March sun had really got in its work, and from under the lip of the drift came an almost inaudible tinkling, the breaking down of the ice crystals that had formed when the first storms came.

Beside me was a balsam, and I took a handful of the needles and rubbed them in the palm of my hand. Now they smelled as needles should, reminding me of the wilderness with its sparkling lakes, its portages and campsites, and a thousand things that played havoc with my peace of mind. It was then I saw the squirrel sunning itself on a branch just above me. Its eyes were closed, but I knew it was aware of my slightest move, for when I shifted my position the white-edged rims opened wide. It stretched itself luxuriously, quivered in a sort of squirrelly ecstasy, loosened up as though it was undoing all the kinks and knots of its muscles.

I strolled along through the back part of the village and there, against a haystack, saw a couple of logging horses shaggy and unkempt from their winter in the woods. They stood, heads down, letting the full force of the sun beat upon their backs. To them this meant green pastures and warmth, the end of nights in a log shelter with the snow banked against the north wind, no more getting out at dawn at forty below to haul the creaking sleighs down the icy tote roads to the cuttings.

On a shed beside the haystack a cat was stretched out, sound asleep. As I stroked its tiger back, it arched against my hand and the soft purring changed to a vibrating rumble from deep within. It was dreaming its own cat dreams of hunting in the long grass of the meadow, of stealing through lush woods in search of young rabbits, of warm, black nights when the whole jungle of back alleys, hedges, and gardens was a tropical paradise.

I had seen enough, and walked back swiftly toward the house, but when I got inside and looked at my typewriter the sun had done its work and planted the seeds of indolence in my soul. In a couple of hours I felt better because the wind turned into a swirling blizzard, the temperature began to drop, and the dream was almost forgotten. But after that first day nothing was quite the same.

It was a month later before I had a chance to steep my senses in the things I'd been thinking about. The snow was gone and the valleys and the meadows were flush with water. The first flowers were out and the hills looked as though someone had taken a great brush and stroked them gently with light green. At the edge of town I found a pond full to the brim with melted snow. Killdeer were calling from the banks and red-winged blackbirds were tuning up in the bushes around it. At the edge of the pond I lay down on a dry hummock of grass with my face close to the surface of the water. Gradually the water grew calm, reflections disappeared, and I distinguished leaves, small pebbles, bits of grass.

A brilliant red water spider crawled up and down a brown

stem. Black diving beetles scuttled everywhere, their tails holding silver bubbles that gleamed like jewels. Then right beneath my eyes cruised a task force of golden crustacea, a fleet of galleons in full sail. The pond was alive with brilliant forms of life which a short month before had been buried in frozen muck. That pool of snow water was their world; a few days of life under the April sun was all they would ever know. Those dazzling golden galleons were doomed as swiftly as they were born.

Leaving the pond, I walked along an old logging road into a stand of aspen and birch, and there I heard the drumming of a partridge. I stalked the sound and saw the bird strutting up and down its drumming log, tail spread, shoulders back until it seemed to be standing upright. Then came the slow, muffled beat of the wings, increasing to a swift crescendo that had in it the booming quality of tom-toms. As I stood there and listened I had visions of what was to come, for that sound was part of many things: trout streams in May, lakes calm in the twilight, hazy afternoons with the smell of smoke in the air, loons calling on the open water.

A little farther on, I found a trickle of a creek, the banks covered with marsh marigold—the flower of the spring floods. The earth was trying its best to cover its soggy desolation while waiting for the green of early summer. The butter-yellow mats that had come so swiftly would hold sway until other flowers began to bloom, adding a note of color and aliveness. But by the time the creeks were back to summer levels, the marigold would be forgotten, remembered only by trout fishermen as bedding in their creels.

I followed the creek for over a mile, until it became a veritable torrent from the water of many swamps and slopes pouring into it. From a hill, I could see where it fanned out into a marsh-grass meadow before emptying into the lake. At this time of year the northern pike were working their way upstream to spawn in the warmer pools of the headwaters. The fish had sensed those waters far down in the icy depths of the lake, and knew that this was the time to follow them to their source.

Climbing down the hill, I stalked the creek cautiously and

sat down on a bank where I could watch without being seen. Then there was a streak across the pool beside me and a thrashing in the riffle. Soon there were other shadows in the pool, and the riffle became alive. Farther downstream in another pool were a dozen pike awaiting the strength to throw themselves up and over the rocks directly above. While I stood there they began, and in a moment the little gorge was churned white with their fighting to get into the pool above them. Clear out of the water they threw themselves, and several were injured on the jagged projecting rocks of the bank. Eventually all worked their way over the obstructions, and the riffle was quiet once more.

Below this spot was a grassy meadow, and there I found them swimming around the tussocks of grass, depositing their eggs in water that was no more than a few inches deep, unaware that in a few days the creek might be down and the precious eggs left high and dry. Some would survive, but hundreds of thousands would perish. The chance was worthwhile, for these waters were warm and there were few enemies and no storms or turbulence. Like the salmon, the shad, and the trout, they were obeying the irresistible impulse to return to old spawning-grounds to fulfill their destiny. The pike swimming around in the long grass of the meadow were completing the age-old cycle.

As I walked back toward home, the grouse was drumming on its log and frogs were tuning up in the little pond. The killdeer were quiet now and the blackbirds had gone to sleep, but I heard the song of the hermit thrush, the clear violin notes that in a little while would make every valley alive with music. Spring in the north *was* worth waiting for and dreaming about for half the year.

No
Place
Between

To the Chippewas that sprawling series of lakes and rivers known as the Kawashaway was a land of mystery. Bounded by brooding stands of pine, its waters were dark, their origins unknown. According to the ancients, the land belonged to those who had gone, was forbidden to those who lived. From the Algonquin *Kaw*, meaning "no," and *Ashaway*, meaning "the place between," it took its name: No Place Between—a spirit land.

Primitive races all over the world have such places, their origins buried in mystery and forgotten legends. Strange things have happened there, and the sense of awe and mystery is always present. The terrain is colored by it, as is everything found there. Some of the old ones understand, and know why this must be, but the young ones laugh and ignore the taboos of the past.

I chose the Kawashaway, now known as Kawishiwi, for the most important expedition of the year, the time when the snow was gone from the ice and the waters from its melting had drained through fissures into the depths below. It was the time when the wilderness of the forbidden land was as alone as it used to be. I wanted to have it to myself so that when I was deep within it I might discover some of the secret of the Chippewas, sense some of the ancient mystery surrounding it. If I did not find what I sought, I still would know the beauty of the country at the time of awakening, when there was a softness in the wind and the long-frozen land was breathing again, expanding and stirring with life after months of cold immobility.

Daylight of a morning in April found me at Silver Rapids, where the waters of White Iron Lake tumbled into the north Kawishiwi. For a quarter-mile there was open water, a long blue gash of it eating its way into the ice. Where it finally ran underneath, there was a rending and lifting that was slowly breaking the main mass on the river. I was afoot, alone, yet there was little danger if one watched the holes and fissures and used care in getting across the open water that now separated the ice from the shore. Only along the paths of the summer portages was the snow still deep. Even here in the mornings before the sun was high the crust was hard enough to walk upon.

Before me stretched twenty miles of brittle frozen surface. My pack rode lightly and the crust was rough enough for perfect footing. What a contrast to the slow, plodding steps of snowshoes! This was sheer joy in movement, and I reached for the clear, open miles ahead.

Gradually the streamers of rose and mauve in the east changed to gold, and then the sun burst over a spruce-etched hill. At that moment the river was transformed into a brilliant crystalline boulevard stretching to infinity. The air was mountain air that morning, and my feet were winged. I was in the forbidden land, land of the spirits, a place to approach with awe and perhaps with prayer.

Within an hour I could see the notch in the hills which marked the first portage. I passed between islands thickly wooded with jackpine and spruce, threaded a narrows choked with the gaunt silver spires of cedar killed by high water, then approached Dead Man's Rapids. I could hear the roar of plunging water long before I could see it. Years before, a lumberjack had been killed there while breaking a log jam. Below was a widening pool, its current gnawing into the blackening fringe of ice along the edges. As I approached, a flock of goldeneyes took to the air and circled widely. The whistling of their wings was a new and pleasant sound. Then they returned and landed with a confident splash in the very spot from which they had flown.

I skirted the weak ice carefully, jumped a moat of open water near the shore, and was on high ground. A few paces back from the rocks the snow was still deep, but frozen so hard I could walk on top. At the other end of the portage I found a high, pyramidal block of ledge—Haystack Rock— stranded in midchannel by the glacial ice. Two more detours around open water and I was again on a stretch of frozen river just this side of the long carry known as Murphy's Portage. How incongruous those names: Dead Man's Portage, Murphy's, Haystack Rock—names of a violent era just passed, axes and peaveys, spiked boots and river pigs, far cry from the sacred ground, the spirit land of the Chippewas.

Now the shores were bold walls of rock, barren, burned over, and desolate. The south shore was still frozen and white, but the north, exposed like a sloping hotbed to the sun, was brown and dry. The leaves and duff looked good to me. I wanted to burrow into the crumbling dark humus underneath, feel it, smell it, and steep myself in its warmth. There was a long stretch of shore without a trace of snow from the edge of the ice to the skyline.

As I worked my way close, the brush cracked and a deer scampered up the slope. Three more joined it, their white flags bouncing and floating over the windfalls. For them that strip of brown earth was a reprieve, a reward for survival. No more deep-frozen trails in the deeryards, no more desperate reaching for cedar twigs, no more starvation at forty below. Farther on I startled a buck and a doe. The buck snorted, wheeled, and sped for the cliffs. Twenty feet at a time, he literally soared over rocks and logs, and scaled slippery ice-rimmed slopes with the reckless and surefooted abandon of a mountain goat. Suddenly there were flashing tails everywhere and then a bold silhouette of the herd against the blue of the sky. During the next few miles I was never out of sight of deer. They had come great distances to feed on that first bare strip along the north shore of the Kawishiwi.

The river now tumbled through a narrow, rocky canyon. Flush and churning golden-brown, it bored its way through gorges and dells, swirled in foam-laced whirlpools, and fought the windfalls and debris of the spring before. Then I was out in the main channel, hiking through a labyrinth of spruce-fringed islands and bays.

A raven flew high above me, circled and circled, watching the lone black figure down on the ice. That crumbling highway was worth watching at this time of year. A short time before, I had seen a deer plunge straight across the narrows, miss the holes and cracks with its slender pipestem legs, and hit the blue water strip near shore in a sparkling flash of spray. I knew the raven had seen it too and the jumps I made as well. The forbidden land was good hunting in the spring.

On the long portage between the river and Snowbank Lake, I found the first hard going. It was late afternoon when I reached the portage, and the sun had softened its crust. To make things worse, two moose had stumbled and plunged down the full length of the trail, pitting it with great uneven holes. Then the shadows lengthened and it was hard to tell which was shadow and which was hole. The two miles were long, and when I burst through the last clump of jackpine it was dark. There was no moon, but the blue-black dome of the sky was bright with stars. The Great Bear hung low, and Cassiopeia and the Pleiades seemed close enough to touch. Ahead was open space for miles. Beyond that, Knife, the Quetico, the roaring Saganagons.

I sat there and rested for a long time. A chorus of coyote howls came from the hills of Lake Disappointment across the bay, and an owl hooted back in the timber. Was there meaning in the Indian paintings on the cliffs east of Insula, in the naming of the Manitou River just over the divide toward Lake Superior? The legends were buried with the last of the old Chippewas. I wondered if I would ever know the spirit land. All I could do was be aware, try to catch something of the sense of awe which once was theirs.

There was movement on the lake, an uneasy whispering, a shoving and a flexing, and ominous groans came from the darkness ahead. I decided not to head out onto the ice, but to follow the shore closely to the trapper's cabin a mile beyond. With a long pole, I moved cautiously onto the ice and slid the point ahead, feeling out the cracks and soft places. In half an hour I was there. The little shelter back in the spruces was still buried in snow and the door covered with drift. A deep, well-beaten, narrow trail led under one corner, and when I saw the board that had been gnawed I knew a porcupine was inside. As I stepped within, it chattered its teeth in the dark beneath the bunk. Then, gathering courage, it waddled past me out into the night. Candlelight and a roaring fire in the little Yukon stove, then supper, fresh boughs, and sleep.

The morning found me hiking down the smooth, wind-polished surface of the lake. In places the ice was covered with frost crystals as big as butterflies and much the same shape. Long crevices were bordered with them, and when the sunlight struck there were flashes of silver and blue and sometimes of flame. Those crystals were the frozen breath of the lake, evidence of its awakening.

A cluster of rocky islands lay to the north, with narrow channels and reefs among them. Trout spawned on those reefs in the fall, and remained until after the ice was gone and the water warmed. Then they moved again to the cold and constant depths of the lake and stayed until the lowering temperatures on the surface brought them once more to the shallows. In those days the season was open in April.

In the lee of an island covered with a stand of pine, I began to chop a hole and discovered that there were still almost two feet of clear-blue ice. When I had finished, I went to the island, cut an armful of balsam boughs, laid them beside the hole, and baited my line with a silver smelt. It was good to lie there in the sun. I studied the shorelines, gazed at the sweep of ice, and watched the sky. Once a wolf, as leisurely as I, crossed between me and the cabin, stopped and looked my way, then disappeared behind a point of land. Ravens wheeled and turned lazily far in the blue.

Just as I hauled in my line for the hundredth time, something took hold and began to move away. I played out line — ten, twenty, thirty feet — and struck hard. The hook set firmly and the fun began: wild dashes around the hole, swirling dives to the bottom, long uncertain sulks. Then, urging the fish toward the opening, I lay with my face close to the water, watching for the flash of ghostly silver. When it came, it startled me — it was so close. The fish must have been just as startled as I, for it made a dash toward the bottom, almost tearing the line from my hand. Then it was up against the ice, five pounds of beautiful trout, enough for several days.

Summer trout from those clear waters are good to look at, but a trout in the spring is a sight to behold — gold and silver with red fins, iridescent in the sun, full bodied, hard and icy cold as the lake itself. I cleaned it carefully beside the hole and left the head, entrails, and backbone for the waiting ravens.

That afternoon I cooked and ate it in the sunshine in front of the cabin, then spent the rest of the day reading Thoreau and making friends with a couple of Canada jays and a red squirrel. The spruces were full of the soft mating calls of the chickadees, the sound which more than any other proves that the sun is warm on the south sides of trees, that spring is on the way. When I whistled the plaintive two-noted mating call they grew excited, flew close to where I sat, tried to find the stranger in their midst.

One day I found a fresh bear trail and followed it back to an abandoned den beneath a windfall. Another time I followed a winding sedge-bordered creek and discovered where a pair of otters had been running and sliding along it, diving under the ice wherever it was broken, only to come out at a new opening for another slide. I saw a big brown beaver sunning itself on a rock close to the water's edge, found the deep furrow it had made to a clump of young aspen back from the shore. The days were full of such adventures, so full that I almost forgot about the ice and that I must leave before the blackening rivers became raging torrents and my glistening highway was gone.

One morning, an hour before dawn, I closed the door of the cabin and left the forbidden land to its crumbling ice and roaring rapids, to its dreams of mystery and of the past. I had not found the secret of the Chippewas, but I had known for a little while the ancient beauties of their solitudes, the warmth of the April sun, a glittering icy highway, and frost crystals as big as butterflies. I had seen the stars very close, had heard the song of the coyotes and listened to the first full breathing of the lake. I had made medicine with the chickadees and the whiskyjacks, had played a game of hide-and-seek with the ravens, had caught a trout and seen its ghostly flash in the blue-black depths of the lake. I had spent some days as leisurely as a bear coming out of its den, soaking up the warmth of spring.

When I thought of all the things I had done, I felt I had known a little of the awe, even some of the fear, that must have been the Chippewas' in their spirit land of No Place Between.

The Loons of Lac la Croix

The loons of Lac la Croix are part of the vast solitudes, the hundreds of rocky islands, the long reaches of the lake toward the Maligne, the Snake, and the Namakan. My memory is full of their calling: in the morning when the white horses* of the mists are galloping out of the bays, at midday when their long, lazy bugling is part of the calm, and at dusk when their music joins with that of the hermit thrushes and the wilderness is going to sleep.

*The foam of rapids and the white plumes of river waves also call to mind "white horses."

But there is a time in the early spring—just after the ice goes out, while the rapids are roaring and the portages beside them half under water, while there are still pockets of snow on shady shores and the entire country is beginning to breathe again—when they really call. Once, years ago on the open reaches of Lac la Croix, I heard them under the light of a spring moon, a wild harmony that has haunted me ever since.

The calling of the loons was only one of several reasons for a trip down the Nina Moose River to Lac la Croix. I wanted to catch some lake trout in the shallows of one of the little lakes on the way in—to feel the fight of them before they had gone into the summer depths, but, more than that, to taste them beside a campfire before they had lost their flavor.

I wanted to see Running Rock again, where the Chippewa warriors tested their strength; to float beneath the painted rocks of Shortiss Island and wonder at the strange pictographs. Above all, I wanted to get the feel of the country at the break-up, to know once more the joy of a paddle in my hands and a canoe slipping along the shores. I wanted to dig my boots into the muskeg and feel the hard granite after months of skis and snowshoes and the white trails of a long winter.

It was midmorning of a day in May when we loaded our packs into the canoe and headed downstream. The river was in flood and the water extended far into the alders and willows of the great bog through which it flows, in contrast to the fall, when rocks were always close to the surface and over the sandy stretches there was barely enough depth to float the canoe. Beaver houses that had once stood high were now almost submerged, and freshly peeled twigs of aspen around them told that their occupants were abroad.

Approaching the first portage, we could hear the roar of the rapids, and we landed high above so as not to be sucked into the current. What a good feeling to throw on the packs and slog down the trail! And what a joy to see that rapids again and hear it rushing through the gorge! After several hours of the portages and winding channels of the river, we emerged at last into Nina Moose Lake.

It was there we saw the first haze of light green over the hills, the budding-out of the aspen. That was another reason for an early trip: to see those slopes in the ephemeral hours before they had begun to darken, while they were still misty and pastel. Grayish-white drifts of the large-toothed aspen and the rose of budding maple made poetry on every shore. One must be on time to see these things, for they do not wait.

At the foot of a riffle, pike and suckers were coming up-stream to spawn and we could almost touch them as they nosed into the current. It would have been easy to snag one with a hook or to pin one down with a forked stick as they thrashed their way over the rocky shallows to the quiet waters above.

We flushed flock after flock of mallards coming into the rice beds above Nina Moose, and I remembered September, when those beds lay golden in the afternoon light and the dusk was full of the whisper of wings. Male redwings perched on reeds and stubs, spreading their wings so that the sunlight caught their crimson epaulets. Grackles flew all around us, their harshness an off-note contrast to the liquid trilling of the rest. Swamps are always a pleasure be-cause there is so much to see and hear, but in the spring, when they are full of sound, they come into their own. We followed the winding, sedge-bordered river beyond, and all the way it was the same — bird songs and running water and the sense of the entire country being in flood.

We navigated a narrow channel with the trees growing close, passed a rocky shelf, and there before us was Agnes Lake, its shores brushed with the same delicate greens we had seen on Nina Moose below. Here we would make our camp, but first there was a trout to catch from a little lake to the west. We paddled to a sandy beach, surprised a couple of deer walking along it, watched their white flags bouncing off through the timber. There we landed, unloaded our packs, and portaged the canoe into a river half a mile away. Another portage and we were drifting down the shore of a small clear-water lake, casting the shallows and rocky reefs with a spinner fly.

Almost immediately there was a strike, and on the light rod we had brought, the trout fought like a rainbow, up to the surface and out, back into the shallows and around the canoe—not as in summer, when they are taken only with heavy tackle from the deeps. We soon had two, a couple of pounds apiece, solid and beautifully colored with the golden browns and reddish tints of the little trout of inland waters. This was enough for the *voyageurs'* feast ahead.

Back in Agnes Lake, we picked up our packs and paddled to the rock campsite near the portage to the Boulder River entrance to Lac la Croix. The flat shelf was now almost flush with the high water, the fireplace nearly within reach of the canoe. We landed and stood there looking over the intimate details of the camp we had left just seven months before: the smooth place under the pines, the tent poles and the pile of rocks beside them, the breakfast place, the log we had left; most of all, we gloried in the broad sweep of water to the southwest.

It was good to make camp again—get the tent up, the sleeping-bags laid out, and a fire under way. We set up the reflector oven, made a pot of tea, prepared the trout. Never had fish been readied with such care or fried with such devotion. When they were the exact shade of golden brown, they were garnished with clusters of red wintergreen berries that had survived the snow. Hot biscuits, a pot of tea, and trout from the icy waters of early spring—who can place a price tag on anything so wonderful? This was worth the anticipation, the extra paddling, and the portages going in and out.

After supper we watched the afterglow and heard a loon for the first time—just a single, lonely, laughing call, but a hint of what might come on Lac la Croix. The stars came out and we sat by the fire watching them, breathing in the smells and the sounds of spring. A breeze came up and waves chuckled against the rocks.

We were up at dawn. The air was cool, and in the stillness little sounds seemed magnified. So still was it that we caught ourselves talking softly. It seemed a sacrilege to use the ax, the first blow against our log so sharp we thought the cliffs must break. We gathered chips and little sticks instead, found a tiny roll of birchbark and a handful of dry pine needles for tinder, laid the fire, and stood at the water's edge.

In the east was a blush of color, and at the mouth of the Nina Moose River a slight movement, an almost imperceptible rising of the mist. A flock of mallards went by on their way to the rice beds. A white-throated sparrow began to sing, its lone, mournful note imparting a flutelike quality to the moment. A chickadee in back of the tent called hesitantly, trying several times before it was sure.

We touched a match to the kindling, and soon the smells of early morning, the damp smells of wet rocks and duff, were joined by the richness of coffee and frying bacon. We sat close, for the air was chilly, and ate our breakfast with an eye to the east and to the mouth of the river. The horizon was brightening now, and at the mouth of the Nina Moose the mists were beginning to move, the horses becoming restive with the rising of the sun. At first they were gray and moved slowly as though afraid to start, but as the east exploded and the level shafts of light hit them, manes flashed silver and they began to run, to crowd one another, and then were in full gallop out of the river toward the expanse of open water.

I had seen them once on the Caribou when sleeping on the flat rock near the outlet. That morning they galloped through the maze of islands to the south. A year before, they were at Chatterton Lake when I was camped at the end of the long rapids. No full view then—only their manes plunging over the white water of the upper gorge—but how they blazed when the full light of the sun burst into the valley. One morning on Knife, when looking down the full sweep of the lake, I watched them come out of the bays where the creeks came in, join together in a great herd, and disappear into the hills. But no place were they better than on Nina Moose. There we could watch them from the start and follow them until they were lost among the trees or ran north toward the open range of Lac la Croix.

We broke camp and shortly afterward made the portage across the swampy trail that leads to the Boulder River. We shot a small riffle that we had portaged the summer before, and then were cruising through a magnificent stand of red and white pine. Old when the *voyageurs* came through, it must have looked to them as it did to us — the tall, straight trunks close to the water's edge, the tops a solid bank against the sky.

On the ridge of a narrow peninsula at the base of Boulder Bay where the river empties into Lac la Croix, we went ashore and walked on the clean, deep carpet of needles. Here was a stand as perfect as any we had seen. At one time a trapper's cabin had been there, a low little structure built of straight logs, its wide eaves close to the duff. Somehow it had seemed a part of that scene, its quiet serenity part of the tall, smooth trunks and the silences of the Bay. I knew Chris Talle, who had once lived there, and knew too the love he had for those pines and for his view down the great waterway of Lac la Croix.

We paddled out to the mouth of the bay, from which we could see the open reaches of the lake. The great surfaces of Running Rock were alive with movement, glittering with thousands of rivulets that spread fanlike over the granite slopes, caught the light, and lost it when they ran over the mosses and lichens and into the crevices. In the old days, so say the Chippewas, young braves started at the water's edge, raced clear to the top a thousand yards or more away, turned there, and ran back to their canoes.

We pitched our camp on a flat, glaciated island, and after supper paddled toward the open lake, where we might catch the moonrise. Just before dusk, with the canoe drifting off the islands, we knew the time had come for the calling, that moment of magic when all is quiet and the water still iridescent with the fading glow of sunset.

Even the shores seemed hushed and waiting for that first lone call, and when it came, a single long-drawn mournful note, the quiet was deeper than before.

Above came a swift whisper of wings, and as the loons saw us they called wildly in alarm, increased the speed of their flight, and took their laughing with them into the gathering dusk. Then came the answers we had been waiting for, and the shores echoed and re-echoed until they seemed to throb with the music. This was the symbol of the lake country, the sound that more than any other typifies the rocks and waters and forests of the wilderness.

The sound of a whippoorwill means an orange moon coming up in the deep south; the warbling of meadowlarks, the wide expanses of open prairies with the morning dew still upon them; the liquid notes of a robin, a rain in the middle west and east; the screaming of Arctic terns in the marshes of the far north. But when I hear the wild, rollicking laughter of a loon, no matter where I happen to be it means only one place in the world to me — the wilderness lake country of the Quetico-Superior.

The feel of Spring

Spring canoe trips into the hinterlands are always exciting adventures after a northern winter, for impressions then seem as fresh as the country itself. One that stands out boldly from the many I have made over the years is a trip young Sig and I took during the war, when he was at home on a last furlough before going overseas with the 10th Mountain Division. I wanted him to carry something special away with him, something he would remember when the going got tough: the feel of spring and the joy of wilderness travel after the break-up.

It was in May, after the ice went out. The sun was shining as though to make up for lost time and the air was full of the smells of thawing earth, open water, and swelling buds. The shores of southern slopes were Nile green where the aspen stood. Ice crystals sparkled on sedges nearby, and in sheltered bays snowbanks still gleamed. The tinkle of melting ice was everywhere. Ducks whispered overhead and sea-gulls wheeled in arcs of silver in the morning light.

"Mountain air," said Sig. "This is the way it feels above timber line."

We stepped into the canoe and pushed off, happy to be paddling again, going into some back country forgotten by everyone except the loons and explorers such as we. Little lakes, creeks, and beaver flowages off the beaten routes beck-oned irresistibly. Seldom seen or used, they were new as the spring was new. The canoe was pointed to the northeast, a chain of boggy waterways south of Knife on the Minnesota–Ontario border. My old friend Jean had told me about them when he heard Sig was coming home, and urged me to take him there to try for trout in one of the clear-water lakes.

"No big ones," he had said, "but they're mighty pretty, sort of a golden, speckled brown with reddish tips to their fins, and rose underneath."

Jean was an outlaw according to the wardens, and one of the finest woodsmen in the north, and what he knew about the maze of waterways in his domain was nobody's business but his own. Like all frontiersmen, he felt the country be-longed to him, was his to use, that trapping was a game and regulations were for outsiders.

"No hard feelings," he told me once. "Those game wardens have to make a living too, and it's their job to keep us out of the beaver country."

The country Jean traveled had always appealed to us, no matter how hard to reach, and going in was a challenge we accepted with delight. Portages were usually overgrown and hard to find, for they did not warrant the time and cost for rangers to keep them open. Beaver sloughs, tiny creeks crisscrossed with windfalls and with barely enough water to float a canoe, strings of little ponds between them — this was the kind of terrain he used.

As we paddled up Moose Lake, it seemed as though we were seeing it for the first time. Spring trips are always that way, and the old familiar route we were following to the beaver country was almost strange. Spring, in addition to many other things, is a time for renewal of memories that may have grown dim during the winter, so when we reached a point on Newfound Lake where Camp 25 used to be, I lingered.

It didn't mean much to Sig, but it did to me. The cabin was gone now. Once it had served as a stopping place for rangers, trappers, and lone travelers. Now it was down, except for a few foundation logs covered with long, brown grass and brambles. A bear had torn one of the logs apart for grubs, and a deer had pawed the earth to get at the salt where the stove had been. I wandered around, remembering bitter winter nights with the stars blazing and the mercury below zero, snowshoe trails leading in, long icicles from the eaves, wolves and foxes hanging from a pole — the winter I made the rounds of the poison trail.*

I could see again the yellow light of the window from the last bend in the trail, sniff the wood smoke and then, when the door opened wide, the warm smell of cooking, balsam boughs, the drying outfit. How bright that lantern used to be, how warm and friendly the cabin after a day in the bush. Everything was gone now with Bill and Jack and Gay and the rest — just a grass-grown mound of crumbling logs.

Sig brought me to with a start. "Let's go, Dad," he said. "We've quite a stretch to make before dark."

We left Camp 25 and passed into a narrows where deer crossed the ice during the winter and often broke through. Once, seven carcasses lay there frozen in the ice, food for wolves, foxes, and ravens. Somehow they never learned, kept coming winter after winter, though the dead lay plainly in sight. Their trail was an old one, and near the water's edge was bare gravel. We went in close, looked down to the bottom, and there in the mud were greenish-white bones.

Just beyond, we surprised a beaver sunning itself on a rock. It blinked lazily, watched us wide-eyed, slid off and slapped its tail. The channel led into a bay and at its end we could hear the Ensign River Rapids. We headed for the sound, fought the current, and landed on a grassy bank — the beginning of our first portage. It felt good to stretch our

*Predator control in the old days by state and federal governments. Poison was used.

legs and feel the rocks under our feet. The river was high and boiling. Fish were coming up to spawn—suckers, northern pike, walleyes—their black shadows holding steady in the flow.

Ensign was calm, its shores as misty green as those on Moose. A partridge drummed, a muffled hidden beat, steady and slow at first, then a swift crescendo, and when it was over the sunshine and quiet were even more intense than before. Halfway down the lake we stopped on a flat, rocky spit to boil a pot of tea.

"Portage out of the northeast end," said Sig, studying the map. "Two or three potholes and flowages and we're on our own."

We spent an hour soaking up the feel of the country, basking in the sun. The whiskyjacks found us swiftly and we fed them bits of bread and meat. A squirrel came down a jackpine and scolded us roundly. Ravens soared, watching the ground below. They knew the best places, the narrows where the deer broke through, the currents between the islands. Nothing ever escaped them. Ours was a sense of golden leisure that comes only in the spring, after months of grayness and cold.

At the end of the lake was a slow, flowing creek separated from the open water by a sandbar. It moved through a swamp grown thickly with sedges, cattails, and alder. A flock of mallards took off from the rushes and the sun glinted on green and bronze as they climbed.

Below the last riffle, we landed and looked for fish but saw none. The portage was low and soggy, and lush buds of marsh marigold showed greenish yellow against the mud. Finding no evidence of a trail, we threw on the packs and canoe and simply followed the bank of the creek. Going up a birch-grown slope we jumped a doe and a fawn, and a little farther on found a beaver pond with a house in its center. We dropped the canoe, pushed into the flowage, and paddled between great silvery boles of tamarack and spruce. Redwings sat on every cattail and shrub, the males flaunting their crimson epaulets and pouring their hearts out in gay *conkaree*s. It was as though all the blackbirds in the north had congregated there that day to make us glad—and never for a moment were they still. This was a sound that comes only in May, when their singing is a warbling symphony to spring.

After the flowage, we portaged through alders and a tangle of willow until we found another widening, where we poled the canoe with our paddles and pulled it forward by holding on to the brush. All the time we were heading east.

"This is Jean's country, all right," said Sig, "exactly the sort of a layout he'd like."

At the far end of the valley we heard running water and went over to investigate. This was different from what we had seen; it was clear, and foaming white where it dropped over a ledge. A school of suckers lay with noses into the flow. We watched as they threw themselves over the rocks onto the ledge, to rest for a moment on their sides, then with a convulsive effort reached the pool above.

Sig reached down from the bow, slipped his hand into the gills of one of them, held it up for me to see. The fish squirmed powerfully and it was all he could do to keep his grip. Black on top, white with a rosy tint underneath, had it not been for the mouth it might have been beautiful.

"How about supper?" he said. "This time of year they're good."

"I'm not proud," I answered, "but let's wait. We're not starving yet."

He lowered the sucker gently into the boiling current and released it. For a while it was quiet, gills opening and closing, then with a lunge it was back in deep water again.

As we lifted the canoe onto the bank, the brush crashed and we glimpsed a black shadow heading up the creek. Portaging, we found several half-eaten fish the bear had been gorging on, as all bears do along the spawning streams of the north. We did not see it again, but heard it beside the creek; it did not want to leave its feeding.

After several portages we finally came onto the shore of a narrow lake about a mile in length. The slopes were rocky and covered with jackpine and spruce, and a spit of a point lay invitingly to one side. A loon called in greeting and the water sparkled in the sun.

"This is it," said Sig. "Here's the lake Jean told you about."

We were alone, with all the time we needed to explore its reefs and shallows, to find where the trout had spawned the fall before. There was no sign of a camp, no tent poles, or a fireplace, or marks of any kind. The site was virgin and unused. I didn't expect to find Jean's set-up in the open for, like all outlaws, he stayed back in the bush, left no telltale trails or ax marks that might give him away. He moved through his domain like an Indian, traveled only at night.

"Come here," said Sig excitedly. "I've found something."

I went over to him, and there beneath a gray, protruding ledge, hidden with moss and pine needles, he had found five rusty beaver traps.

"Here is the proof," he said. "This is his country."

He placed the traps back carefully under the ledge and covered them with moss.

The sun was down now, the lake beginning to glow. We built a fireplace out of the greenish-gray slabs of slate near the water's edge, pitched the tent as close to the fire as we dared, with a view down the lake. We could watch the fire before going to sleep, and would waken with a vista before us. Such things were important to us, though of course there was the hazard of a gale blowing sparks from the fire, or even of snow and rain, but those we were willing to face.

After supper the dusk settled quickly and the loons called as they always do south of Knife: long, rolling peals of laughter from every point of the compass, merging at last into a weird, continuous harmony that somehow epitomizes the spring break-up better than any other sound. There was magic in the air, and in the morning we would know if what Jean had said was true. It was good to lie there in our bags watching the glow of our dying fire and the deeper glow of sunset beyond; but most of all it was good to feel the ground again and to know we were back in a country we loved.

The day dawned clear, and as the sun burst over the ridges to the east we were bathed in its warmth. We cooked breakfast, assembled our gear, picked out flies and spinners on a chance the trout would be near shore. Anything could happen, there might be no reefs, the fish already deep. We followed the north side, casting the shallows all the way, but not a strike did we get.

"Might be too early," I said. "Sometimes they don't hit for several weeks after the ice goes out."

I wanted so desperately to get some trout for Sig's sake, but try as we might, nothing took hold. At the very end of the lake was a rocky peninsula, almost an island, with a shallow gravel reef between it and the shore. If ever there was a spot, this was it. If the trout had spawned there in the fall, they must still be close—but each time we drifted through it was the same.

We changed lures and went deeper, but all we caught were snags. By midafternoon a wind came up out of the east, clouds covered the sun, and it grew cold. We landed on the rock beside the reef and built a big fire out of windfalls. The gale increased and suddenly there was a drift of snow in the air. Once more we tried the shallows with the same result, then paddled back to camp without a word.

We tightened the tent ropes, cut a good supply of wood, got ready for the storm. The chickadees stopped their singing, squirrels and whiskyjacks disappeared, and by the time we crawled into our sleeping-bags the ground was white. For a long time we lay watching the flames, and went to sleep with the sound of snow and sleet hissing into the coals and whispering against the frozen tent.

Spring in the north is strange and wonderful and always full of change. We thought of the long paddle back, the slippery portages with an icy wind over the open reaches toward home.

"The sun will be out tomorrow," said Sig. "It's got to come out."

"It will," I replied, but I knew better with the blow coming out of the east.

Several inches of snow fell during the night and in the morning it looked like November. The water was leaden, the new green of the aspen-covered slopes now a bank of white.

It was bitterly cold, the wind high, so we built up the fire, and I made a breakfast for explorers who needed strength and courage to face the day: porridge, bacon, eggs, bread, and plenty of hot coffee. As we basked in the warmth our spirits rose and we both had the same idea.

"Listen, Dad," said Sig, "there were a lot of dry logs on that rock. We could paddle over there, get a real blaze going, dash out to the narrows, fish for a while and come back to get warm."

"Besides," I told him excitedly, "this change of weather might just start the trout feeding. Sometimes this is all it takes."

We put on all the clothes we had, fought the waves to the ledge, and in a short time had a roaring fire under way. When we were thoroughly warmed again we pushed the canoe into the narrows and over the reef we had tried the day before.

Sig's first cast brought a strike and a good one, and I watched him land that fish as though I had never seen it done before. This would tell the story. The trout fought hard, raced under the canoe, went down and surfaced once. Tiring, it came close. I reached down and lifted it into the canoe. A beauty it was, golden brown with reddish fins, a decided blush of color along the sides. We hooted with joy and laughed as the snow swirled around us. By that time we were both so numb we were forced to return. Another log, and the blaze went high. We slapped our hands together, pummeled each other roundly, and soaked up the heat until we were ready once more.

This time it was my turn, and in a moment I had one as beautiful as the first—only a couple of pounds, but as hard, firm, and well colored as any trout I'd seen. Again we sped back to get warm.

The next time we both fished, hooked two trout at once and got our lines so hopelessly snarled it took an hour to get them untangled. By noon we had all the law allowed, paddled back to camp happy as two *voyageurs* could ever be. We had found our little lake and the trout Jean had told us about. What is more, we had caught them in a howling snowstorm on flies and spinners.

That night we celebrated and each of us had a fish for supper, knowing they would never taste so good again. Trout fried to a golden brown, hush puppies in the fat, a can of beans and tea. We piled logs on the fire and crawled contentedly into our bags. The storm could howl now and we didn't care. Tomorrow was another day.

In the morning we took down the frozen tent, packed the outfit, and started down the creek the way we had come, slipping and sliding over rocks and windfalls, snow whipping our faces from the brush. A smooth, rocky slope we had come over easily was treacherous now, and once I fell with the canoe. Another time we crossed a rocky stream bed, its boulders covered with a smooth, unbroken blanket of white. Each step was a gamble, a chance for a broken leg or a sprained ankle.

But paddling was the worst, with gusts of snow and spray freezing onto our clothes, until it was hard to bend our arms. Mitts were of no use and our frostbitten hands took a beating. At each portage we stopped to build a fire, and several times debated whether to go on or to pitch camp until the storm had blown itself out. Only one hitch to that: Sig was soon due at Camp Hale and the end of his furlough was near. So we abandoned any thought of giving in, fought our way down mile by frozen mile, past Camp 25, down Newfound and the full sweep of Moose.

By late afternoon we were at the landing at the south end of the lake where our cruise had begun four days before. We unloaded, went back to the water and stood looking down the lake. White-flecked combers and blowing drift were out there. Then the sun burst through a rift in the gray, scudding clouds and for a glorious instant the waters were blue again and the shores dazzling with silver and Nile green. We looked at each other and laughed. We had won, found what we had gone in for—the feel of spring—and had some trout as proof. We had known the thrill of exploring forgotten country together, and had seen it at its best.

The Storm

It was mid-April before I heard the first robin, the fluid, haunting melody of gurgling notes which sounds like the flowing of water itself. As yet, the grass had not begun to green, but there had been mist and a soft lushness had come into the air which spoke of more to come.

The snow was all but gone now; only in the deep, shaded valleys and on the north slopes was there any sign at all. Some of the smaller lakes had opened, but the larger ones were as solid as they had ever been. The ice was blackening, and at the mouths of creeks and rivers there were long blue V's of open water. The song of the robin meant many things to me: getting up early and listening to the birds; long walks through the woods to the headwaters of trout streams, with the sun bursting over the tops of trees and the underbrush sparkling with dew. It meant the sharp pungence once more of the low places at dusk; the flaming of the dogwood stems along the creeks; the reddening of the maples and the bursting of their blooms long before the leaves. It meant pussy willows in every swamp, white drifts of them against the brown of the still frozen bogs; it meant the Nile green that would brush the poplars and, with the pearl-gray masses of the large-toothed aspen, make each hillside and valley a pastel dream.

The robin meant the end of many things — of ski trails, and rabbit tracks, and the beds of deer in the snow. Life had changed suddenly and was full of a new excitement. From that time on I was a scout and a spy, spending every waking moment anticipating the smells, sights, and sounds of coming events.

That same day I took a long walk over a field to the south of my home. The grass, now rid of snow, was matted and covered with grayish mold. Everywhere were the tunnels and the round grass houses of the meadow mice. Small pools of ice-cold water lay in every hollow, and I knew that some of them were full of larvae and crustacea and other forms of life which until then had lain dormant in the muddy bottom. Before me was a sky-blue pool larger than the rest, a permanent pool with enough moisture during the summer so that cattails, sedges, and willows grew around its edges. Then came a sound that quickened my heart — the resonant *quack-quack-quack* of a mallard hen, the contented talk of ducks who have found good pasture. Not since October had I heard that sound, a breath out of the past which brought memories of rice beds golden in the sunlight, of flocks swooping out of the sky, and of sunsets when the long, trembling V's laced themselves against the afterglow. Then, of a sudden, three mallards took to the air — a drake and two hens — and climbed high, the sunlight catching the color of wing bars, the pearl gray of undersides, a splash of bronze. It was over in a moment, and I watched as they headed into the north.

As I left the pond I heard a killdeer — *kill-dee-kill-dee-kill-deeeee*. For me, no other sound of early spring so completely catches the spirit of thawing earth and running water as this one call. Even more than the robin, more than the mallards, this wild, clear call epitomizes the break-up and the great migration wave to come. I watched a pair of them circling the pool, caught sight of them later running over the field, and always *kill-dee-kill-dee-kill-deeeee.*

Then I caught a flash of white wings high in the blue and heard the distant crying of seagulls heading north from Lake Superior. I knew where they were going. Although the big lakes were still frozen and would not be free until early May, there were open spots on the rivers and on the smaller ponds. They knew and were heading back to stake their claims on the little rocky islands that would be their nesting places all over the Quetico-Superior.

Toward the end of April there were many birds: the white-throated and white-crowned sparrows in droves, the song sparrows, the black-headed Harris, and many others. The yard on top of the hill was full of them — chickadees, juncos, and evening grosbeaks by the score — but what really brought music to the hill were the purple finches. The feeding stations were never without them, and at one time we counted a dozen full-colored males. There were robins and pine siskins and redpolls, and the music of all of them at dawn was something to hear. Never before had there been so many at one time during any migration period I could remember. They came in late April and stayed on, for the days were warm and the buds swelling fast. In sunny places the brownish-purple catkins of the alder hung heavy with pollen. The maple flowers flushed into crimson along the edges of the swamps, and the pussy willows turned gold with dust. In sheltered places the grass began to green, and the creeks were gurgling and full to the brim. The days continued sunny and warm, and as soon as one group of birds moved out another took its place.

Then one day in May the sky darkened and, instead of rain, snow began to fall, lightly at first and then in huge flakes, until the brown earth was turned to white. The birds stayed on and other flocks came in, swelling their numbers, as they met the storm raging over the border country. The first day the snow covered all the food in the countryside.

And still the flocks came in from the warm and rainy south just a short flight below. When the birds ran into the storm front, they stopped and joined those who had waited.

I shall never forget the morning of the second day with the snow still coming down: the sound of the singing at day-break, the warbling of the purple finches, the mating calls of the chickadees, the song sparrows, the robins, and the clear flutelike calls of the whitethroats all blended into one great symphony of thrilling sound while all the time the snow grew deeper and deeper.

Surely, I thought, the storm would not last. The sun would come out and it would disappear swiftly, but instead the cold grew more intense, a wind came up, and the snow came down as heavily as before. By the end of the week there was a foot of it, and the singing grew less and less notice-able. The birds sat dejectedly wherever there was shelter, and I picked up many that had died. Their feathers were sodden with the wet, and though I had placed out all the food I could find—suet for the chickadees, bread crumbs, chick feed, sunflower seeds—the birds were thin and ema-ciated. Now without fear, they gathered in droves around the feeding stations, but they grew weaker and weaker, and more and more of them died as the storm continued.

Then came the grackles with their opaque eyes and long, sharp bills. I did not actually see them kill any of the smaller birds, but they did feed on those which had died and fright-ened those still alive. At the first flash of black wings all birds on the hilltop froze. There was no move to escape, just complete immobility as they waited for death to strike. The grackles would stay for a while, then leave as quickly as they had come. As soon as they were gone, the singing would begin once more in spite of the terror the birds had known.

The storm covered the north country with from twelve to sixteen inches of snow; millions of birds were stopped in their migrations, and uncounted thousands must have died. Then the skies cleared, the sun came out, and in a week the ground was almost clear. The rivers were in flood now and the pools larger in the fields. The still-unfrozen buds went into fuller and fuller bloom, and the grass turned swiftly into green to make up for the delay. The birds kept on singing and began to move off toward the north.

I remember getting up at dawn one morning after the storm was over. There again was the music, swelled by new species that had just come in. The purple finches, the grosbeaks, the whitethroats stayed longer than the rest, and their singing never ceased. The blizzard of May and all that it had brought were forgotten. Then came a day of warm rain and all the snows were washed away.

I listened to the robin in the tall aspen where I had heard it first, and it poured out its liquid trill as happily as before. A pair of brown thrashers came into the yard, as they have for many years, and sang from the top of a tall birch tree, imitating every bird around them and some they had heard in the south. They began their long hopping surveys, around and around the house, their cinnamon tails bobbing up and down. The house wrens moved into their old nest and announced to all strangers that the yard was theirs and theirs alone. The threat was gone, spring and its dangers past.

The
Sound
of
Rain

One night in my tent I listened to the rain. At first it came
down gently, then in a steady-drumming downpour, and I

lay there wondering when I would begin to feel the first
rivulets creeping beneath my sleeping-bag. The deluge continued, but there were no exploring trickles, no mist through
the roof of balloon silk. The tent, on the little rise with its
thick cushion of bearberry, had perfect drainage all around,
and the ropes were tied to two good trees. The gale could
blow now and the rain come down, but I would be safe and
dry the rest of the night. I settled down luxuriously to enjoy
a sound I had known on countless campsites in the wilderness.

Like all woodsmen, I had planned for the morning, had
tucked a roll of dry birchbark and a few slivers of pine under
one end of the canoe. My packs were in one corner of the
tent, the ax handy just in case something snapped during
the night. The canoe was snubbed to a rock well up from the
shore.

The wind came up and the tent swayed, but the ropes
held; in the rain they grew taut as fiddle strings and the
tent more waterproof with each new assault. A branch
swished close and two trees rubbed against each other. The
woods were full of sounds, creakings and groanings, with
branches dropping from the trees.

How much good the rain would do, how fresh the water
in every stream, how flowers would pop with the sun, the
linnaea, the anemones, the dogwood and everything else
along the trails! The ferns on the rocks would begin to grow
again, and the silvery caribou moss would be soft and
resilient with just a tinge of green. The dry and brittle lichens
along the cliffs would turn from black to velvet green. Mushrooms and toadstools would suddenly emerge from every
dead log, and the dusty humus would bring forth growths
that had been waiting for this very hour, for no rain had
fallen in a month.

The coming of the rain soothed a longing within me for
moisture and lushness after the long-continued spring
drought. As I lay there, I too seemed to expand and grow,
become part of the lushness and the rain itself and of all the
thirsty life about me. This is one of the reasons I like to hear
the rain come down on a tent. I am close to it then, as close

as one can be without actually being in it. I have slept in many primitive shelters, under overhanging cliffs, in lean-tos made of spruce boughs and birchbark, in little cabins roofed with poles and sod. I have slept under canoes and boats and under the spreading branches of pines and balsams, but none of these places gives me quite the feeling I get when sleeping in a tent.

The drops are muffled by the cloth, none of the staccato drumming there is under a hard roof. Once I slept in a cabin with a tin roof and listened to a chorus that night that was too violent to enjoy, a mechanical sound as though a thousand drums had broken into a rolling crescendo all at once.

Not long ago I met an old friend, C. K. Leith, one of the world's most famous geologists. He had been a professor of mine, and for a time I had worked under him on the Wisconsin Geological Survey. After his retirement he had served as a consultant to the government, using his great knowledge of the world's minerals to guide exploration and development.

We sat in the Cosmos Club in Washington, D.C., one rainy afternoon talking about the old days, the days in the bush when he was a legend of endurance and fortitude, of the treks he had made into the far north that even today are contemplated with awe and wonderment by hardened prospectors. He was eighty-two when I talked to him last, but still as straight and energetic as ever. Suddenly he was quiet, and a faraway look came into his eyes as he sat watching the rain spatter down into the courtyard.

"Do you know where I'd like to be right now?" he said finally. "In my old tent somewhere, safe and dry with nothing to do but listen to the rain come down."

He smiled and I knew he was cruising the back country of the Canadian Shield, down its brawling rivers, across its stormy lakes, knowing again the feeling of distance and space, the sense of the old wilderness.

"As you get older," he said, "and more involved with world affairs, you lose that life. But those were the good old days for me."

When I heard of his passing, I knew that somewhere back

in the bush he was listening to the rain come down and that he had found again the life he loved.

In the woods of Listening Point, the drops soak into the ground as they should, stopped by an intricate baffle system of leaves and pine needles, small sticks and bits of bark, the partly decayed vegetation just underneath, and finally the humus itself, rich, black, and absorbent, the accumulation of ten thousand years. Here in the north it takes over a thousand years to form a single inch of it, and if the glacier receded from seven to ten thousand years ago, the humus on the Point has taken just that long to form.

Below the humus is the mineral-rock soil, the result not only of the grinding of glacial ice but also of the gradual breakdown of the granite and schist and greenstone by the frost and rain, the action of the acids of countless roots, the burrowing of hordes of insects and worms and beetles. This layer rests upon the native ledge, but by the time the rain reaches it, it has slowed and soaks into it without loss. There are no rivulets except where the rock is bare, no erosion or run-off to the lake. All that falls stays there and moves into the water table of the area to be held in reserve.

It was good to lie in the tent knowing the rain was replenishing the water supply, that none of it was being lost except where it ran off the smooth rocks, that even between them, in every cleft and crevice where there was any accumulation of humus at all, it would be held for months to come.

I awakened once during the night. The muffled drumming was gone and there was only a steady dripping from the trees, a sort of settling down and rearranging of the entire moisture pattern. I went to sleep almost immediately and didn't wake until dawn. The sun was shining then, and the little bay was heavy with mist. I stepped out of the tent and looked at a clean world. Every needle glistened, the rocks shone, all the debris of a month of dryness had disappeared. The Point looked scrubbed and shiny too. I took my little roll of birchbark and the kindling and started the fire, made a cup of coffee and fried some bacon, but decided before I began any work I must walk down the trail to see what had happened along the shore.

The trail was lush and the needles beaten flat. Many leaves lay there, for in the wind and rain all those not strong enough in their holdfasts had fallen to the ground. Many little twigs and branches had been beaten off by the purging storm. Only the live wood had been strong enough to withstand it. Mushrooms and fungi were pushing through the humus, and one shaped like a whitened hand groped skyward with delicate fingers.

On a stump was a tiny patch of painted lichen, each silver tip brushed with carmine. A mossy log beside the trail now bloomed with linnaea, the tiny flowers bell-like twins, none of them over a quarter-inch in length. There were literally hundreds of them covering the bright-green moss of the log. I knelt down, buried my face in them, and caught one of the subtlest odors in the north. Scientists call them linnaea for the famous Swedish botanist, Linnaeus, who first named them in the north of Sweden. He loved these little flowers, and it is significant of his feeling that the best-known painting of him shows one in his hand.

That patch of linnaea had a special significance after the rain, for it seemed to epitomize the resurgence of growth in all the area. The tiny flowers were part of June, part of late spring, and their odor presaged all the smells to come. This also was part of listening to the rain come down, for in the listening was the feeling that all life was responding to the moisture, all forms benefitting and growing in the night.

I have always been fond of linnaea because it grows in the shadows, away from the direct glare of the sun, seems a part of big timber and the depths of the wilderness, a spiritual relative of the orchids that are also found there. How different from the harebells growing on the cliffs in the direct sweep of the winds, flaunting their blue and wiry beauty to space. They can stand the searing dryness of midday heat, do not need the rains. The linnaean bells are shy and delicate, would shrivel to nothing if protection were gone or the rains did not come in time. As fragile as solitude, they would disappear at the slightest intrusion.

Farther down the trail, in a patch of aspen and birch, I found a late-blooming cluster of hepatica. Of a sudden I was a boy again in the cut-over country of north Wisconsin, looking for the first flowers of spring. There the ground was covered with them, whereas here they are almost rare. The rain had brought out several blooms, the same sky-blue petals against their sturdy clumps of fuzzy, flattened leaves that I had known years ago. I smelled the almost hidden fragrance of the past, but more than the smell was the way those waxen petals turned toward the sky. Someone told me long ago they were bits of blue fallen to the earth, and to a child that was the truth. No ordinary blue was this, but the kind one sees in early morning after a rain and before the sun has gained its brilliance.

On a little side hill above the swale was a patch of dwarf dogwood not yet in bloom. Soon the entire hillside would be stippled with the four white, notched petals typical of all dogwoods on the continent. Up here only two or three inches in height, they make up for their lack of size as soon as the blossoms fade, for each produces a cluster of brilliant red berries that transforms the place of their growing from late summer until fall.

I had one more place to go, the swampy spot below the ridge. That was where a lady slipper grew, so I left the trail and worked my way down into the boulders where open water now stood between the rocks. On a little shelf with a deep cushion of pine needles and well away from the dampness, I found a single bloom, just as I had a year ago on the cliffs of Crooked Lake to the north. Down in the closed canyon of Crooked that day it had been breathless and still. No wind stirred the water, and even the birds seemed weary with the heat. Wanting to get away from the closed-in feeling of the lake itself, I had climbed high onto the cliffs above the painted rocks. On a great shelf carpeted with moss I rested, enjoying the panorama of wilderness far below me, the sweep of distant ridges with sky-blue waterways between them. Just then I happened to look down to the mossy shelf below, and there in the shade made the discovery of the day: a single pink lady slipper in full bloom. While I looked at it, I forgot the heat and humidity and thought of the great woods to the south, where its closest of kin, the showy lady slipper, is found and of all the great solitudes of the earth where members of the orchis family bloom. Alike in their needs, no matter where they grow, in the depths of tropical jungles or in the woods of the north, they have shadows and solitudes as part of their lives. They are flowers of the primeval and the unchanged places of the earth.

My lady slipper just off the Point was part of all that, as were the linnaea and the rest, part of the old wilderness I had known, part of the beating of rain on the tent the night before and of the lushness and fullness that had come with it.

Witching Hours

It was dusk, and the loons, hermit thrushes, and white-throats were almost through with their calling. The tapered line unfurled and a fly soared over the rushes, landing like a puff of down upon the water. It sat there a moment, then seemed to struggle to free its wings before taking to the air. A swirl, and the fly rod bent, and soon the bass swam in slow wide circles beside me.

A swish of the net and it was inside, its red gills opening and closing, its tail beating a soft tattoo against the bottom of the canoe. Then again the rhythmic moving of the rod, the quiet drifting along the shore. My friend turned to me then from the bow, and in his eyes was the light of magic.

"The witching hour," he said.

I knew what he meant, for this was one of the times when the lake evoked a spell, when it mirrored not only the shores but the spirit as well. Through some strange alchemy that water possesses during such witching hours, we absorb its calm, its mystery or violence as though we were a part of it.

Millennia of living along seacoasts, lakes, and rivers, beside ponds and springs and water holes have had their influence. Man's history is woven into waterways, for not only did he live beside them, but he used them as highways for hunting, exploration, and trade. Water assured his welfare, its absence meant migration or death, its constancy nourished his spirit.

A mountain, a desert, or a great forest may serve man's need of strength, but water reflects his inner needs. Its all-enveloping quality, its complete diffusion into the surrounding environment, the fact it is never twice quite the same and each approach to it is a new adventure, give it a meaning all its own. Here a man can find himself and his varied and changing moods. No wonder the Psalmist said: "He leadeth me beside still waters/He restoreth my soul."

I have never forgotten my friend and our paddle in the dusk, and though he has been gone a long time, I still remember the almost mystical look in his eyes when he turned to me from the bow of the canoe and said, "The witching hour."

I have cherished those hours, watched and waited for them no matter where I have been. On Listening Point there have been many, and on distant waterways far beyond I have learned the signs and symbols that announce them. Sometimes they come without warning, mere flashes of the hours they might have been, but whatever their length, even the faintest intimations are worthwhile.

The following morning I was at the rocky tip of the Point and, as always, the past came back to me with smells and sounds and feelings I had known: Basswood Lake, when the islands rested like battleships in the mist; Lake Superior, when its fullness threatened to overflow its shores; Kahsha-piwi, when the waters trembled between the cliffs; and many more. Most vivid of all was the memory of a dawn on the Camsell River between Great Slave and Great Bear, far to the north. Why, out of all that complex of half-forgotten memories, this one should stand out more boldly than the rest, I do not know, but in a flash I was on a ledge close to a swirling pool.

The east was reddening, a churning rapids and a falls above, and those below tinged with color—the air surcharged with the vast excitement of plunging water. How pungent the smell of the fire that morning, how sharp its crackling, how good the cup of coffee before its blaze!

There was no thought then of the rapids we must shoot, the portages ahead, or the miles we might have to paddle on stormy lakes. In the aliveness and poetry of that breaking day, nothing was impossible. We were part of a great river flowing toward the Arctic Sea, at one with its surging power and beauty.

By midmorning, a spanking breeze brought out the whitecaps. The sky was cloudless, the water blue, the air fresh and cool—a day for action and exploring. We launched the canoe, headed into the teeth of the wind, and fought the waves toward a point of land a mile away. Skirting the rocks with their spouting plumes, we landed in a protected little bay, climbed the slope to a level spot among the spruces, and watched the waves roll in and dash themselves against the ledge below.

Though marching combers may pin you down for hours, and you may be windbound on an exposed, rocky point for days at a time, if the sun is shining and your captors are blue and topped with silver spray it is no hardship, for the waters are full of song. When the rapids glint and their shouting is glad and free, the treachery of hidden rocks and ledges is forgotten, and the canoe moves in and out with a sureness born of the bright spirit that comes from them. Running before a gale, when spume is white and blowing in the wind and the water is in a sparkling champagne mood, is no time for somber thoughts. On such days you can shout and sing to the wind, for witching hours are there for the taking.

The magic of these days came back and the joy of glittering movement was in me.

But when there is no wind or the faintest intimation of a breeze and all the roughness of the water is erased, when reflections are so stark and clear it is hard to tell them from the shores, all thoughts of action disappear as well. Even so, there is witchery at work, though its magic is of a different kind. At such times it seems word has been passed that nothing should be done, and those who would move faster than in a dream do so at their peril. Paddling becomes difficult then, packs on portages double their weight, and everything is slowed to the pace the lake has set.

It was so on Mirond, its long unbroken reaches extending endlessly toward the south, and on the great Wollaston when mirages on the far horizons played tricks with eyes and one could not tell whether the shores were five or forty miles away. It has been that way on Sturgeon and Rainy and countless times on smaller lakes, when canoes seem to be floating high above the water and thoughts drift with them in an all-engulfing quiet that penetrates minds as well as bodies. There is no opposing such vast placidity, for like a cloud it flows around you. But if you allow yourself to become a part of its languor you may know the witchery of complete abandonment.

Calm may also mean the gathering of forces long held in leash. On one such day at Listening Point, when the lake was as still as it had ever been, magnificent thunderheads piled high and moved across the sky, but there was no movement underneath. Not a leaf or a blade of grass stirred, and there was not a ripple on the surface of the water. A yellow light hung over all the land and under its glow was uneasiness and fear. Everything was placed under cover, the canoes well back in the trees, firewood beneath the eaves, whatever could blow away made fast. Flashes of lightning came from the thunderheads, and rolling peals of sound. Ducks flew madly past the Point into the protection of the river mouth and then came back again. Birds dashed swiftly into cover and songs were hushed. A squirrel crouched quietly between a huge branch and the trunk of a pine, sat there cowed and waiting for the storm.

A slick smoother than the rest showed off the Point and it was yellow with the light. A school of minnows skittered like bursting bubbles across its surface as a great pike rolled lazily where they had been. Loons ran across the water and their calling was wild and uncontrolled. Seagulls coasted far out from shore and for once their mewing was stilled.

Now it seemed quieter than before, and an ominous sound of rushing came from everywhere at once. Trees swayed on top of the ridge and then along the shore; in a moment the lake was full of angry waves and they were crashing against the rocks. Thunder rolled, a bolt of lightning struck a pine on a far hilltop, and a dead aspen crashed to the ground nearby. Norways swayed and bent as the earth beneath them lifted and trembled.

Then came the rain, and with it hail. The water was churned to froth and the ground became white. I sat inside the cabin and watched the assault of the storm against the Point, with its pines and tall, brittle aspen, looked out at the tossing combers and the spray as they hurled themselves against the ledges. The rain streamed off the eaves, then settled down to a slow and steady drumming; as I listened, the wind died and the vast gray wetness of the lake absorbed all violence. Then it was over—only the dripping from the trees onto the sodden moss and brush.

I stepped outside to survey the damage. The ground was strewn with branches, the shoreline littered with needles and debris. Suddenly the sun burst out from behind a black, scudding cloud and sprayed the shore with the glory of its light. Gulls flew high, silver breasts gleaming. Squirrels chattered, harvesting the cones that had fallen to the ground. A whitethroat sang, rather haltingly at first, grew brave, then whistled loud and clear.

A strange and complex witching hour, it had been a combination of many I had known, of twilight and dawn, of calm and violence, and even of gaiety toward the end.

But of all the moods, all the variations of feeling and experience the waters of a lake can give, it is moonlight that is most remembered, for here is a strange excitement born of man's long and intimate involvement with this light. There is mystery when paddling down the gleaming avenues between islands silhouetted against its glow, unreality in the colonnades of tall trees or in the silvery reeds reflected in the shallows. My memories are full of it: cypress swamps in the south with their hanging festoons of Spanish moss, little ponds gleaming like silver medallions in dark timber, the full glory of an unbroken path of it down one of the great waterways of the north, a castle moat in England shining like polished pewter.

At Listening Point it seems best when watching the moonrise from the high rock, seeing its first glimmer over the ridge and its slow, majestic emergence, pulsating and trembling, until at last the huge orange ball is free of the horizons, grows high and white to clothe the Point and all the lake with its enchantment.

These witching hours blend one into the other as calm may blend into storm, for water reflects not only clouds and trees and cliffs, but all the infinite variations of mind and spirit we bring to it.

Silence

It was late May, before dawn and the first calling of the birds. The lake was breathing softly as in sleep; rising and falling it seemed to me, absorbing like a great sponge all the last sounds of spring: the tiny trickles, the tinklings and whisperings from still-thawing banks of hidden snow and ice. No wind rustled the leaves; there was no lapping of water against the shore, no sound of any kind. But I listened just the same, straining with all my faculties toward something — I knew not what — trying to catch the meanings that were in that moment before the lifting of the dark.

Standing there alone, I felt alive, more aware and receptive than ever before. A shout or a movement would have destroyed the spell. This was a time for silence, for being in pace with ancient rhythms and timelessness, the breathing of the lake, the slow growth of living things. Here the cosmos could be felt and the true meaning of attunement.

I once climbed a great ridge called Robinson Peak to watch the sunset and to get a view of the lakes and rivers below, the rugged hills and valleys of the Quetico-Superior. When I reached the bald knob of the peak the sun was just above the horizon, a flaming ball ready to drop into the dusk below. Far beneath me on a point of pines reaching into the lake was the white inverted V of my tent. It looked very tiny down there where it was almost night.

Watching and listening, I became conscious of the slow, steady hum of millions of insects and through it the calling of the whitethroats and the violin notes of the hermit thrushes. But it all seemed very vague from that height and very far away, and gradually all these merged one with another, blending in a great enveloping softness of sound no louder, it seemed, than my breathing.

The sun was trembling now on the edge of the ridge. It was alive, almost fluid and pulsating, and as I watched it sink I thought I could feel the earth turning from it, actually feel its rotation. Over all was the silence of the wilderness, that sense of oneness which comes only when there are no distracting sights or sounds, when we listen with inward ears and see with inward eyes, when we feel and are aware with our entire beings rather than our senses. Sitting there, I thought of the ancient admonition "Be still and know that I am God," and knew that without stillness there can be no knowing, that without divorcement from outside influences man cannot know what spirit means.

One winter night I stood in wonderment beneath the stars. It was cold, perhaps twenty below, and I was on a lake deep in the wilds. The stars were close that night, so close they almost blazed, and the Milky Way was a brilliant, luminous splash across the heavens. An owl hooted somberly in the timber of the dark shores, a sound that accentuated the quiet on the open lake. Here once again was the silence, and I thought how rare it is to know it, how increasingly difficult ever to achieve real quiet and the peace that comes with it, how true the statement "Tranquillity is beyond price."

More and more do we realize that quiet is important to our happiness. In our cities the constant beat of strange and foreign wave lengths on our primal senses drives us into neuroticism, changes us from creatures who once knew the silences to fretful, uncertain beings immersed in a cacophony of noise that destroys sanity and equilibrium.

In recognition of this need, city churches leave their doors open so that people may come off the streets and in the semi-darkness find the quiet they need. I know a great sanctuary whose doors open onto one of the busiest and noisiest streets of the world. I go in there whenever I pass, and as the doors close behind me and I look up to the stained-glass windows and in the dusk sometimes hear the muted chords of a great organ, the quiet returns and I sense the silence once more. Beneath that vaulted dome is a small part of the eternal quiet the outside world once knew.

In Winchester Cathedral in England is a stained-glass window dedicated to Izaak Walton, patron saint of all anglers. In the base of that window are four words which embody the philosophy of all who enjoy the gentle art of fishing and the out-of-doors: STUDY TO BE QUIET.

They are the key to all he ever wrote and thought about. Beside the rivers Itchen and Dove, Izaak Walton fished for peace and quiet, sought the silences and the places where thoughts were long and undisturbed.

Silence belongs to the primitive scene. Without it the vision of unchanged landscape means little more than rocks and trees and mountains. But with silence it has significance and meaning. What would the Grand Canyon's blue immensities and enormous depths, its sense of timelessness, be like with a helicopter roaring the length of it?

John Muir said: "The sequoias belong to the solitudes and the millenniums." Those ancient trees, some of which were old before the birth of Christ and mature long before the continent was discovered, have among them the stillness of the ages. They are more than trees; their very existence is sobering to short-lived man.

What would the wilderness lake country of the Quetico-Superior be like with the roar of airplane motors and high-powered transportation engulfing it? The charm of a canoe trip is in the quiet as one drifts along the shores, being a part of rocks and trees and every living thing. How swiftly it changes if all natural sounds are replaced by the explosive violence of combustion engines and speed. At times on quiet waters one does not speak aloud, but only in whispers, for at such moments all noise is sacrilege.

In this land of wilderness waterways there are special places where the silence seems deeper and more inclusive than elsewhere. One of these is a camp on a small island above the Pictured Rocks on Crooked Lake, a rocky, glaciated point looking down a narrow channel banked by a high cliff on one side and a mass of brooding timber on the other. Each night after supper was over, the canoes and gear stowed away, we used to sit on the end of the point to listen. As the dusk descended, the loons filled the narrows with wild, reverberating music, but it was when they stopped that the quiet came. The great mass of the cliff on one shore and the gloom of pines on the other seemed to cup and hold the silence until we were enveloped by a dark curtain that stifled all thought and feeling.

When the loons began again it was as though their calling slashed the curtain like a knife, only to have it close and be as darkly mysterious as before. Here was a deep awareness of ancient rhythms and the attunement men seek but seldom find. More than temporary release from noise, it was a primordial thing that seeped into the deepest recesses of the subconscious.

Once, in the Kluane country of the Yukon, I found a different kind of silence. We had climbed to the rim of a great bowl to look for Dall sheep. All around were snow-covered ranges and peaks, before us an enormous amphitheater. We sat there several hours and watched the scattered bands moving undisturbed below the rim.

After a time I left my companions and walked toward one of the closest groups of ewes and lambs feeding some three hundred yards away. I crossed a low ridge and was alone. It was as though I had walked through an open door and closed it quietly behind me. Nearby was a bank of ice and snow, brown and discolored with windblown dust. A ground squirrel chittered from its burrow and small brown birds that looked like siskins twittered and flew around the edge of the ice, feeding on the seeds of grasses and flowers that had bloomed a month before. The twittering in that engulfing quiet was almost loud. Never before had those tiny flutelike notes seemed so distinct and clear.

I remembered the lines of Robert Service, bard of the Gold Rush days:

I've stood in some mighty mouthed hollow
That's plum full of hush to the brim.

I realized then this was what he meant — here the mighty-mouthed hollow, plumb full of hush to the brim, the sense of enormous and crushing silence that lay over all that great land.

How often we speak of the great silences of the wilderness and of the importance of preserving them for the wonder and peace to be found there. When I think of them I see the lakes and rivers of the north, the muskegs and tundras beyond all roads. I see the mountain ranges of the west, the Yukon, Alaska, and the high, rolling ridges of the Appalachians. I picture the deserts of the southwest and their brilliant panoramas of color, the impenetrable swamplands of the south. Physically they may always be there, their beauty unchanged, but should their silences be broken, their true meaning will be gone.

Young Ottertail

As I sat on the end of Listening Point watching a flaming spring sunset and looking toward the northwest and the wild country of Lac la Croix, a day's paddle beyond, I thought of the legend of young Ottertail. Why I thought of him just then I do not know, except that the moment was one of mystery and my mind ranged to far places that spoke to me of mood. Such a place was Pine Point on Pickerel Lake, north of the Canadian border, the burial place of a young Indian of the Lac la Croix band.

One moonlit night I was camped there, and it was then I heard the story of how, long ago, an Ottertail of the Chippewas had carried the body of his son through miles of wilderness and laid him to rest in the most beautiful spot he knew. There among towering red pines he buried the youth who would have been the poet of his tribe, the boy who someday would have put into song the longings and legends of his people.

When death swooped down on the Indian village at the mouth of the Snake River and took him away, the father knew he must find a spot where the spirit would be at peace; and, because the boy loved great trees and a song was always in his heart, he chose the cathedral pines on Pickerel Lake.

Two days by canoe from the village, he laid the body to rest in a shallow grave at the very end of a tremendous colonnade of Norway pines. Over the grave he built the traditional shelter of bark and cedar, leaving an opening at one end so the spirit could come and go at will.

Legend has it that on nights when the moon is full and birds are wakeful with its light, the spirit of young Ottertail leaves its resting place and walks among the pines down to the sand beach on the west shore of Pine Point. There it stands and gazes toward the village of Lac la Croix.

When the waters are still and the moonlight more than beautiful, the spirit may even leave the point, drift across miles of wilderness toward the home it once knew. It was seen watching for sturgeon below the first falls of the Snake, and another time a phantom canoe moved among the calling loons of Lac la Croix, a canoe that never left the loons and never came to land, just drifted there—and then, like a morning mist, faded from view. Just before dawn it was seen floating like a wraith along the edges of muskegs where they came close to the water.

There are some who have seen it in the rice beds in September, a lone canoe always at dusk or at dawn, with the rice sticks beating rhythmically and the canoe moving through the rows of bundled stalks, clear to the end of the rice field and back again, when all the other canoes were at the parching or in the woods hunting and no new people had come in.

There are some who swear they have seen it on the portages where the rivers come close to the trails, for all of these places young Ottertail loved. With the coming of dawn, the spirit is always back at Pine Point, and there it rests until the coming of the next full moon.

As I sat there watching the burnished gold of the horizon change to mauve and blend with the water, I wondered if the spirit were again on its way. The moon had risen behind me, and even before the color was gone from the west it was silvering a path through the iridescence of the afterglow. On such a night his spirit might be stalking through the checkerboard of gloom beneath the pines or standing on the beach looking back toward the Indian village.

It might be moving up the Indian Sioux out of La Croix into the Vermilion; then, floating over the lake, it might descend the Tamarack as Indians have always done to the mouth of the river, not two miles off Listening Point. The spirit land of the Chippewa, the spirit lands of all peoples — how important to catch their meaning, how little we know when we see only rocks and trees and waters, mountains and meadows and prairies, how impossible to catch the feeling of any country without sensing its legendry and the mystery of what cannot be seen, places that always speak of the unknown.

There are many places close to Listening Point that have this feeling of mystery; one is Darkey Lake, which Indians never cross without hushing their voices. Darkey is far more than a good trout lake, more than a link in the route to Brent and the country to the east, far more than the outlet of the Minn River to Martin's Bay of Lac la Croix. These are part of the physical terrain that all travelers know, but the mood and feeling of the lake, the knowledge that here the spirits dwell, give it poetry.

Not long ago I passed that way. The day was glowering, the wind holding out of the southwest. We fought our way from the eastern entrance through the whitecaps, down to the cliffs with the pictured rocks, sat below them in the lee and studied the great serpent of the horned head with the canoes paddling beside it, the moose showing the tracks of hunters on either side, the lichen-covered figures no longer plain enough to understand. As we sat there under the wild scudding clouds and their spattering of sleet, I could not help but feel that ghostlike canoes were there beside us.

The Kawashaway country of "No Place Between" is another such area just to the east of Listening Point, a no-man's-land of the past, a portion of the spirit world that was once part of the lives of Indian tribes long gone.

The upper reaches of Kawnipi also speak of unknown things. On Massacre Island, at the mouth of the Wawa-wiagamak, a battle took place many years ago. Old guns have been found there, baskets for the making of maple sugar, and the remains of an old encampment. I never slip into the river's mouth without being conscious of the past, without wondering what happened there.

But mystery drawn from personal associations may be as powerful as that of long ago, the feeling that in certain places old friends are still alive and happenings in your own life are as vivid as before. Such a place is the mouth of the Range River where it empties into Low Lake, on the route from Burntside to Jackfish Bay of Basswood Lake. With a friend now long gone I spent many happy days there, and when I stop at the campsite we used, I find things still unchanged. There in a cleft between the rocks was where we stored our extra food and cooking outfit, there the grassy shelf where we rolled our bags when the weather was good and the sheltered spot in the jackpines when gales blew out of the north. Not long ago on a night when the snow was spitting and ice forming in the shallows, I was there alone, but the past was with me and my friend was young and full of laughter and we were gay as we listened to the storm.

There are many places that even without legendry or personal associations speak of mystery. Such a spot is a broad shelf of rock just back of the Point, a little glade tucked into the woods away from the lake. No trees are there, but over the rocks is a thick carpet of caribou moss and blueberry. I sat there in the moonlight once and it seemed as though all the voices of the woods spoke to me, as they always do in glades, wherever they might be. There is something about a glade when the moonlight filters in and trees are black against the sky and you have the sense of being in a great room that speaks of unseen things. A horned owl hooted while I was there and birds chirped sleepily, and as I listened, it became a place of magic and the world was far removed. In such a place the wilderness holds meanings far beyond what it has in the light of day. There young Otter-tail might have stood looking toward the Indian village at the mouth of the Snake on Lac la Croix.

At another place just south of the beach huge boulders stand among the pines. In among them is a powerful sense of the primeval, and those enormous blocks of stone make me feel as though great forces are all about me, and I can feel the moving of the ice sheet that dropped them there ten thousand years ago. So I felt at Stonehenge one night in England, and in the Druid circles on the high downs, where men of the past had communed with the unknown.

There are many places which have mood, places which, because of a combination of physical circumstances, have a character all their own. I think of Glacier Lake up the Fauquier chain from Louisa to the Saganagons River, the campsite at the far east end where you can look down its full length to the portage in the west. Somehow Glacier, with its high, almost mountainous shores, gives one a sense of space and removal, a feeling of unlimited distance and the unexplored. Though an old canoe route traveled by many, it has never lost its character. Standing there at dusk and looking down that long, mysterious expanse, I feel it must go on and on, that beyond it are places men have never been.

On the way to Glacier Lake, between Burke and Sunday, is a shallow stream known as Singing Creek. This outlet of Sunday Lake ripples over stones, is shaded with cedar, and from the campsite beside it is a vista of the waterway above. I never camp there without being a part of its music. There laughter comes easily, for there is no sense of the primeval or the unknown. It is a place for banter and fun, and songs are as natural as those that come from Singing Creek itself. To lie there at night and listen to the chuckling of the water means happy dreams. There is no mysterious sense of the past, but poetry there is, and a mood that sings.

The sun was down and the moon high, the night growing chill. The Point was part of the legendry of the north and all its moods. In time it would grow into all the places I had known and would build for me a legendry of its own. What mood it would have in the years to come depended on what happened there and the joys and sorrows that would weave themselves into its rocks and trees and vistas and be as much a part of it as they.

Summer

*Summer begins in June. It comes after the wild
excitement of spring, the migration of birds,
their mating and choosing of places to live
and defend. It is a time of fullness and
completion, the goal of all that has gone
before, a time of feeding the young on the
clouds of insects, on the hosts of worms and
grubs in the fertile humus and new fruits with
which the earth is now blessed. All living
creatures gorge themselves and their young
on the food that is at this season so rich
and abundant. It is a time for building
strength and storing energy for whatever may
come. It is also a time of joy.*

*In the warmth of rains and sunny days, the
forest floor literally teems with life. Seeds
swell and burst and grow, colored fungi and
lichens all but spring from the ground.
Flowers are bolder in their hues than those
of spring. They bloom in crannies on cliffs,
on bare rock faces, in swamps and forest
shades. Dwarf dogwood stipples the ground,
drifts of pink linnaea lie beneath the pines,
while cherries and plums lace woodland
borders in fantastic designs. There is a
sense of almost tropical lushness after the
stark severities of winter.*

*Because there is so much of everything, there
is a relaxation in effort and even time for
playing in the sun. In the mornings the mists
roll out of the bays, pink when the days are
bright, ghostly white when they are dark.
In the evenings the loons call, while hermit
thrushes and whitethroats warble in the
aspen.*

*This is the essence of summer—a time of plenty
and a soft green beauty in which hardships,
survival, and eternal striving belong to a
different and almost forgotten time.*

The Way of a Canoe

The movement of a canoe is like a reed in the wind. Silence is part of it, and the sounds of lapping water, bird songs, and wind in the trees. It is part of the medium through which it floats: the sky, the water, the shores.

In a canoe a man changes and the life he has lived seems strangely remote. Time is no longer of moment, for he has become part of space and freedom. What matters is that he is heading down the misty trail of explorers and *voyageurs*, with a fair wind and a chance for a good camp somewhere ahead. The future is other lakes, countless rapids and the sound of them, portages through muskeg and over the ledges.

If the morning is bright and sparkling, canoes seem like birchbarks freshly gummed for the rapids and winds ahead, and we are *voyageurs*, bronzed and bearded and burned from wintering in the Athabasca country. We are on our way to Grand Portage to meet old friends, to eat fresh bread again and to dance to the fiddles in the Great Hall,* to fight

*The main building of the North West Company post at Grand Portage.

heroic battles and do the things we can boast about for a year to come. There are songs in the wind: *"En Roulant ma boule,"* *"La Belle Lizette,"* and *"La Claire Fontaine."* In the sound of the wind we can hear them.

A man is part of his canoe and therefore part of all it knows. The instant he dips a paddle, he flows as it flows, the canoe yielding to his slightest touch, responsive to his every whim and thought. The paddle is an extension of his arm, as his arm is part of his body. Skiing down a good slope with the snow just right comes close, with the lightness of near-flight, the translating of even a whisper of a wish into swift action; there, too, is a sense of harmony and oneness with the earth. But to the canoeman there is nothing that compares with the joy he knows when a paddle is in his hand.

A rowboat has the fulcrum of the oarlock to control it, and the energy of a man rowing is a secondary force, but in paddling the motion is direct — the fulcrum is the lower hand and wrist, and the force is transmitted without change or direction. Because of this there is correlation and control. There is balance in the handling of a canoe, the feeling of its being a part of the bodily swing. No matter how big the waves or how the currents swirl, you are riding them as you would ride a horse, at one with their every motion.

When the point is reached where the rhythm of each stroke is as poised as the movement of the canoe itself, weariness is forgotten and there is time to watch the sky and the shores without thought of distance or effort. At such a time the canoe glides along obedient to the slightest wish and paddling becomes as unconscious and automatic an effort as breathing. Should you be lucky enough to be moving across a calm surface with mirrored clouds, you may have the sensation of suspension between heaven and earth, of paddling not on the water but through the skies themselves.

If the waves are rolling and you are forced to make your way against them, there is the joy of battle, each comber an enemy to be thwarted, a problem in approach and defense. A day in the teeth of a gale — dodging from island to island, fighting one's way along the lee shore of some windswept point, only to dash out again into the churning water and the full force of the wind, then to do it again and again—is assurance that your sleep will be deep and your dreams profound.

One day on Namew we faced a powerful northeaster coming straight down the lake. Quartering immediately, we soon found ourselves riding against enormous rollers with broad troughs between them, the canoes coasting down one incline and up the other, almost lost in the process. Had it not been for the breadth of those intervals it would have been impossible to make headway. Attempting to pass a low, swampy island, for a long hour we barely held our own. Over and over again we battled to the hissing crests of the waves, slipped over their tops, tobogganing down the slope with enough momentum to climb the next ridge.

For a time we lost the other canoes, then saw one far to the right, a tiny silver speck miraculously making its way in the teeth of the gale. A swift glance behind and there was the third topping a crest, only to disappear in its depths. Two hours later we made the far shore, had some tea and bannock, stretched out on the flat limestone and waited for the wind to die.

There is a satisfaction in reaching some point on the map in spite of wind and weather, in keeping a rendezvous with some campsite that in the morning seemed impossible of achievement. In a canoe the battle is yours and yours alone. It is your muscle and sinew, your wit and courage, against the primitive forces of the storm. That is why, when after a day of battle your tent is pitched at last in the lee of some sheltering cliff, the canoe up safe and dry, and supper under way, there is an exultation that only canoemen know.

Almost as great a challenge is running with the waves down some lake where the wind has a long unbroken sweep. Riding the rollers takes more than skill with a paddle; it takes an almost intuitive sense of the weight and size of them and a knowledge of how they will break behind you. A bad move may mean that a comber will wash the gunwales. A man must know not only his canoe and what it will do, but the meaning of the waves building up behind him. This is attack from the rear without a chance of looking back, a guessing at a power and lifting force he cannot see. But what a fierce joy to be riding with a thousand white-maned horses racing with the wind down some wild waterway toward the blue horizon!

It was that way on Amisk, the wind a great hand on our backs. Hissing combers were around us and it was every canoe for itself, no chance even for a side glance to see what was happening to the others. Carefully quartering to the southeast and toward the end of a long gleaming point blood red in the sunset, I was conscious of each wave, judging its power and lift by the sharpness of the approaching hiss. If we skirted the point too close we might hit submerged rocks, if we went out too far we could be carried into the open lake with its twelve-mile sweep and miss our chance of turning into the shelter behind it.

The cliffs were still a couple of miles away. Only the tip of the point was flaming now, the base a dull, angry red fading into the blackness toward the west. The canoe would ride a great roller, slip off its crest, and in that moment of cascading down the slope of the trough we would start quartering. In the blow on Dead Lake the sun had been shining, the combers sparkling and alive. Now in the near-dusk they were dull and gray, the valleys in between bottomless and black. Like running a rapids in poor light, you depended on the feel.

Every third or fourth wave was bigger than the rest and I could sense its lift long before it struck. When it caught us the canoe would rise swiftly, then hurtle forward like a great spear into the spray. The cliffs were much closer now, their lower parts brushed with black, only the top and very tip of the point still colored. All I could think of was a red knife sticking out into the blackness of the east, its tip alive, its blade and handle darkening into purple. We were quartering successfully and would miss the stiletto's end, but what was in its lee we did not know. Could we land there, or would we find the same precipitous cliffs we faced? We would have to camp there even if we had to climb to their tops.

.   .   .

Rapids, too, are a challenge. Dangerous though they may be, treacherous and always unpredictable, no one who has known the canoe trails of the north does not love their thunder and the rush of them. No man who has portaged around white water, studied the swirls, the smooth, slick sweeps and the V's that point the way above the breaks has not wondered if he should try. Rapids can be run in larger craft, in scows and rubber boats and rafts, but it is in a canoe that one really feels the river and its power.

Is there any suspense that quite compares with that moment of commitment when the canoe heads toward the lip of a long, roaring rapids and then is taken by its unseen power? At first there is no sense of speed, but suddenly you are part of it, involved in spume and spouting rocks. Then, when there is no longer any choice and a man knows that his fate is out of hand, his is a sense of fierce abandonment when all the *voyageurs* of the past join the rapids in their shouting.

While the canoe is in the grip of the river, a man knows what detachment means; knows that, having entered the maelstrom, he is at its mercy until it has spent its strength. When through skill or luck he has gone through the snags, the reaching rocks, and the lunging billows, he needs no other accolade but the joy that he has known.

Only fools run rapids, say the Indians, but I know this: as long as there are young men with the light of adventure in their eyes and a touch of wildness in their souls, rapids will be run. And when I hear tales of smashed canoes — and lives as well — though I join in the chorus of condemnation of the fools who take such chances, deep in my heart I understand and bid them "Bon voyage!" I have seen what happens when food and equipment are lost far from civilization and I know what it takes to traverse a wilderness where there are no trails but the waterways themselves. The elements of chance and danger are wonderful and frightening to experience and, though I bemoan the recklessness of youth, I wonder what the world would be like without it. I know this is wrong, but I am for the spirit that makes young men do the things they do. I am for the glory that they know.

But more than shooting white water, fighting the gales, or running before them is the knowledge that no part of any country is inaccessible where there are waterways with portages between them. The canoe gives a sense of un-bounded range and freedom, unlimited movement and exploration, such as larger craft never know. Sailboats, rowboats, launches, and cruisers are hobbled by their weight and size to the waters on which they are placed. Not so a canoe. It is as free as the wind itself, can go wherever fancy dictates. The canoeman can camp each night in a different place, explore out-of-the-way streams and their sources, find hidden corners where no one has ever been.

Wherever there are waterways there are connecting trails between them, portages used by primitive man for count-less centuries before their discovery by white men. Although overgrown and sometimes hard to find, they are always there, and when you pack your outfit across them you are one of many who have passed before. When you camp on ancient campsites, those *voyageurs* of the past camp with you.

The feeling of belonging to that tradition is one of the reasons canoemen love the sound of a paddle and the feel of it as it moves through the water. Long before the days of mechanized transportation, long before men learned to use the wheel, the waterways of the earth knew the dugout, the skin hunting-boat, the canoe. A man feels at home with a paddle in his hand, as natural and indigenous as with a bow or spear. When he swings through a stroke and the canoe moves forward, he sets in motion long-forgotten reflexes, stirs up ancient sensations deep within his subconscious.

When he has traveled for many days and is far from the settlements of his kind, when he looks over his cruising outfit and knows it is all he owns, that he can travel with it to new country as he wills, he feels at last that he is down to the real business of living, that he has shed much that was unimportant and is in an old, polished groove of experience. Life for some strange reason has suddenly become simple and complete—his wants are few, his confusion and uncer-tainty gone, his happiness and contentment deep.

There is magic in the feel of a paddle and the movement

of a canoe, a magic compounded of distance, adventure, solitude, and peace. The way of a canoe is the way of the wilderness and of a freedom almost forgotten. It is an antidote to insecurity, the open door to waterways of ages past and a way of life with profound and abiding satisfactions. When a man is part of his canoe, he is part of all that canoes have ever known.

The
Portage

The portage lay in the end of the bay, and there a battered
white sign was nailed to a tree. As the canoe slipped beside a
log we stepped into the shallows and lifted out the packs.
The sign was broken in half, torn no doubt by a curious bear,
weathered and beaten by the wind, but on it were the names
of *voyageurs* who had gone before.

I stood for a long time looking at that sign as I have looked
at hundreds in the wilderness lake country here and far to
the north, and marveling as I always do that somehow I had
arrived at a known and definite point on the map. That

morning the portage had seemed far away from Listening
Point. There had been miles of open water, narrows, and
islands to traverse, and now, at last, here it was exactly
where it was supposed to be.

The trail was narrow, no more than a foot in width, for,
like animals, men in the wilds make little paths. It was
carpeted with pine needles and the leaves of aspen and birch,
packed hard by the feet of generations of travelers. It led
between rocks, around hummocks, skirting wet places, using
logs for bridges where the muck was soft, over windfalls and
around clumps of blocking trees. This primitive path was
part of the great network that laces together the waterways,
a connecting link between two lakes, but in its simplicity
and the way it threaded through the woods it was typical
of all the wilderness trails in the world.

The first man who found his way through here had followed perhaps the trails of moose or caribou, for they also
travel from lake to lake, but because they seldom follow the
shortest route he was forced to branch off and head for the
closest point of the shore. No doubt he climbed a tree or a
ridge to get his bearings, then returned and blazed his way
or broke off branches to guide him back.

The next man through followed the marked trail with
more ease, broke more branches, slashed a few more blazes
on the trees, might even have cut a windfall blocking the
way. From then on each traveler improved the portage a
little more until at last it was as definite and direct as the
terrain would allow. After many years of use, someone with
more ambition than the rest chopped out the great logs that
men had scrambled over and finally tacked a sign on a tree
near the water so that canoes coming in would see it from
the lake.

This portage was primitive as all such trails are, the result of steady improvement by all who came that way, and
dedicated to a kind of use that belonged to the wilderness.
To straighten out the bends and loops that had become a
part of it because of obstacles avoided, to remove all natural
hazards and even to mark it too well would have taken something from it, just as an old, winding road changes in char-

acter when all the curves are eliminated in the interest of speed.

For countless thousands of years men have followed such trails. It is instinctive to pack across them, and you bend and weave, adjust your weight and balance, do all the things your subconscious experience tells you to do without realizing exactly what is happening. In the low places your feet feel for the rocks and tussocks of grass, for the sunken logs that keep you from bogging down. You approach them as a horse approaches a bridge, with the same awareness of danger. Over the rocks and beside a rapids, where a slip might plunge you into a torrent or over a cliff, your feet are your eyes as they have always been where the going is rough.

I have known portages all over the country, the short, unimportant ones not rating a name, the difficult ones oftentimes of great historic interest. There is Grand Portage, once gateway to the northwest, the nine-mile carry around the brawling rapids of the Pigeon River where it empties into Lake Superior; Staircase Portage just above, where *voyageurs* built a rugged stairway down a steep cliff; Frog Skin Portage from the Churchill to the Sturgeon Weir, where the Crees as a mark of derision stretched a frog skin and hung it there to show those who had not learned to stretch a beaverhide that this was how it was done. The legends about them are many, for it was here men met on the long routes they must follow in the north.

I thought of these things as I tossed the canoe onto my shoulders and started across the portage. Countless feet had trod it smooth long before I came. During the logging days part of it had been used as a tote road, but now it was grown to brush and trees again. It was a long carry and uphill most of the way, and I thought I could make it without a stop, but near its crest I weakened, placed the bow of the canoe in the crotch of a birch, and rested. Then, almost imperceptibly the trail led down the ridge, and it was there I caught the first sight of blue—just a glimmer through the trees but enough to take away the weariness and fill me with the same old joy I had known thousands of times in the past, an elation that never grows old and never will as long as men carry canoes and packs along the waterways.

In spite of the labor, it is this that makes portaging worthwhile. There is no substitute. If someone transports your outfit for you, it is lost. It colors your entire attitude, makes each lake reached mean infinitely more. It is exactly like climbing a mountain. You could be dropped there by helicopter or view it from a low-flying plane, but unless you have climbed cliffs, scaled precipices, and inched your way upward, fighting for breath, you have no understanding of the satisfaction of the first long look into space. So it is with portages and the first sight of glorious blue through the trees. When I dropped my canoe at last into the water and stood there puffing and blowing and looking down the expanse of the lake, my feeling of accomplishment was one that had been earned.

But just walking across a portage has its compensations too. In a canoe, even though you slip quietly along the shores, you cannot achieve the feeling of intimacy that is yours on the ground. There you hear sounds that are lost on the water, see things that until then have been hidden. After hours of paddling, a portage brings new muscles into use, and how delightful to rest with your back against the canoe, doing the aimless things one does when there is nothing to think about and rest is the greatest luxury on earth.

Such an interlude I had at the end of the McAree Portage, where I sat and idly scuffed the moss with the toe of my boot. I felt something hard and, thinking it might be a root, kicked it loose. To my surprise, it was an old knife, heavily rusted, with the horn handle partly gone. I scraped off the rust and there was the mark IXL, one of the trade knives carried by Indians and *voyageurs*. Dropped perhaps during a meal or after skinning a beaver, there it had lain until I kicked it free. That knife is now in my cabin, a reminder to me not only of the days of the fur trade but of the delight of a resting place on the portage from McAree to the island-studded reaches of Lac la Croix.

No one in the Quetico-Superior country has arrived, however, until he has made the Kahshapiwi Portage, a mile of the most rugged terrain along the border. It starts from Yum

Yum Lake and is fairly level at first, then goes down into a swampy beaver flowage where in spring the water may be waist deep, and afterward over a high and mountainous ridge. The view from that ridge of the knifelike gash that is Kashapiwi and its high shores, with the realization that only those who are willing to take the punishment of that grueling trail may see it, is reward enough.

Some lakes have short portages between them, such chains often becoming major routes. Between these, however, are waterways unknown and unexplored. An itinerant hunter or trapper may have worked his way into them, but a blazed trail without continual use grows swiftly back to brush and trees. Sometimes when exploring it is necessary to cut a trail into one of these waters off the known paths of travel—an experience modern canoeists may still enjoy. In the early days, before aerial surveys and photographs and before dependable maps were even dreamed of, there were many blank spaces where the country was a challenge.

Of all the portages I have known, the one I most often dream about when I am far from the canoe country is along a knifelike ledge of rock between two gorges on the Saganagons. On my first trip down that river I camped there on a tiny level shelf of rock on a night that was full of the thunder of rapids and falls on either side. That place made such an impression on my young mind that it has become endowed with mystery and I have only to close my eyes to hear its music. But there are many more, those that wind between the boles of great trees and those with far vistas from the highlands with their smooth, glaciated rocks like pavements through the woods. There are short, delightful ones—merely interludes between the paddling—and long, hard ones from one watershed to another. But always they are gateways to adventure, meeting places for *voyageurs*, punctuation marks between the long, blue sentences of lakes across the maps.

Stream
of
the
Past

To recapture the spirit of any era you must follow old trails, gathering from the earth itself the feelings and challenges of those who trod them long ago. The landscape and way of life may have changed, but the same winds blow on waterways, plains, and mountains, the rains, snows, and sun beat down, and the miles are just as long.

When I first saw the wilderness lake country of the Quetico-Superior, I knew little of its frontier days beyond the fact the logging was about over, the great booms, rafts, and enormous mills gone. Lumberjacks were still around with their stagged high-water pants and the swagger that belonged to them alone. So to me the frontier period seemed part of the time in which I lived.

Even the Indians were not entirely of the past, for some stopped at old campsites, fishing and traveling the lakes and rivers as they used to do. Their social system and spiritual beliefs were changing; reservations had been established; areas they once roamed, limited. I did not associate this with the past, simply accepted things as they were. I was familiar with the heroes of pioneer days, but they were legendary with an unreality that had nothing to do with the present. So it was with the meager accounts I had learned at school of the fur trade, the early settlements along the St. Lawrence River in Quebec, names like Champlain, Cartier, Radisson, and Groseilliers, and the spread of exploration toward the west.

Not until I began guiding in the region the French *voyageurs* had traveled did I begin to sense its color and history. I came to know some of the descendants of these men, who gave me my first living picture of the past. Joe Bouchard, Leo and Henry Chosa, Pierre La Ronge, and others told stories they had heard as boys of great birchbark canoes that came down the border from far-off Montreal, leaving such names to lakes, portages, and rivers as Lac la Croix, Deux-Rivières, Grand Marais, and Maligne. Until then I had taken French names as a matter of course, but now they had meaning.

I learned about Grand Portage, the great carrying place on Lake Superior where thousands of Indians, *voyageurs*, and traders gathered each summer to exchange axes, knives, and muskets for the priceless pelts of beaver—the most famous rendezvous on the continent, the halfway point of a canoe route 3500 miles in length where brigades from Montreal met those from Fort Chipewyan, and until the early nineteenth century the most vital funnel in the trade and exploration of the northwest. From this isolated wilderness encampment, well known in the courts and banking houses of Europe, expeditions sallied forth to Rainy Lake and Lake Winnipeg, and by way of the Saskatchewan and Churchill rivers to Fort Chipewyan at the far west end of Lake Athabasca.

Grand Portage was one of the longest and most rugged portages of the entire route, with its long miles of hills and swamps around the impassable Pigeon River, a trail that tested the strength and endurance of generations of French *voyageurs*. Alexander Mackenzie of the North West Company, famed for his discoveries, described them: "I have known some of them to set off with two packages of ninety pounds each and return with two others of the same weight in the course of six hours, being a distance of eighteen miles over hills and mountains." He might have added that some even carried three.

I read the Mackenzie, Vérendrye, and Thompson diaries and through them caught at last the flavor, romance, and danger of the days in which they lived. The great highway of lakes, rivers, and forests extending along the Minnesota-Ontario border became alive, and when I paddled down the waterways, ran the rapids, and made the portages those old canoemen had trod, mine was a sense of personal identification so powerful and real, it seemed as though I were actually one of them.

Their story of the two hundred years between 1650 and 1850 was a dramatic one in which fortunes in furs and supplies moved up and down the great highway. It was a time of struggle, warfare, and piracy between the rival fur companies of England, France, and the United States. A vast network of forts and posts was established throughout the north and west, and as a result the lands were opened up, bringing settlers and development in their wake.

All this was fascinating to a young guide, but it was the *voyageur* who captured my imagination, he who carried the tremendous loads, paddled from dawn to dark fighting waves and storms, existing on a diet of pea soup and a daily spoonful of fat. His muscle and brawn supplied the power for all the exploration and trade, but in spite of the harshness of his life, the privation, suffering, and constant threat of death by exposure, drowning, and Indian attack, he developed a nonchalance and joy in the wilderness which have never been equaled in man's conquest and exploitation of any new land. These gay French Canadian canoemen with red sashes and caps, singing in the face of monotony and disaster, were the ones who stood out.

For several years I guided with a young French Canadian, Pierre La Ronge, in whose veins ran the blood of a long line of *voyageurs*. From the very first he called me François, and no sooner were we together than we spoke in the patois of Old Quebec, from where his people came. The longer this went on the more we acted and felt like the men from Montreal and Trois-Rivières; after a while, we felt more like *voyageurs* than guides of the twentieth century.

"Pierre," I might say, "when you go for catch dose trout, use hangerworm or hoppergrass."

"Oui, oui, François," he would reply in mock desperation, "dere ees no hangerworm or hoppergrass een dees countre. All we have eese copper spoon"—and, with a gesture of utter bafflement any Quebecer might envy, "What can poor Pierre do?"

When cooking the inevitable dried fruit he would announce to an invisible audience, "De prune ees de fines' berry dat grows een de swamp."

A ridiculous performance, perhaps, but it provided many laughs, and talking like men from the villages along the St. Lawrence somehow colored our attitude toward the life we were leading and gave all events, including the weather, a humorous twist.

If someone in the party happened to balk at the weight of a pack, invariably he would be reminded of the standard load for *voyageurs*, the regular 180 pounds of the two packets he had to carry, and of the great La Bonga who put them all to shame with five—a total of 450 pounds. The carrying then was done with a tumpline, a broad leather strap over the top of the head. In those early days of guiding, before I had seen the kind of carrying still done by Indians and halfbreeds back in the bush, I used to wonder if the old stories were true. Now I know they were, for I have seen what tumplines can do where carrying loads is an accepted thing.

The *voyageurs* entered the service young, learned by doing, and gloried in their strength. Portages were a relief from paddling, a place for visiting and feeling the ground under their feet after the hazard of rapids and the waves of big lakes. Pierre and I were no different, and when after a long paddle we finally hit the shore, we tore into the packs as though each was a personal challenge. Sometimes when the weather was foul and the trails a soggy mess, Pierre would quote from William Henry Drummond, the bard of the fur trade:

De win' she blow on Lac St. Claire,
She blow den blow some more,
Eef you don't drown on dees beeg lac
You better kip close to shore.

But the poem he loved best of all was "The Voyageur." He knew all the verses and sometimes at night, when all the work was done and the time had come to crawl into our blankets, he would load up his blackened pipe, light it with a coal, get to his feet, and begin. All would go well until he came to the last verse; then his eyes grew round and dark and his voice husky as he declaimed:

So dat's de reason I drink tonight
To de men of de Grand Nor'Wes',
For hees heart was young, an' hees heart was light
So long as he's leevin' dere —
I'm proud of de sam' blood in my vein,
I'm a son of de Nort' Win' wance again —
So we'll fill her up till de bottle's drain,
An' drink to de Voyageur.

But the gaudy brigades are gone now, no longer are retipped paddles flashing in the sun, no more the singing and the sound of voices across the water — nothing left but crumbling forts, old foundations, and the names they left behind them. There is something that will never be lost, however: the voyageur as a symbol of a way of life, the gay spirit with which he faced enormous odds, and a love of the wilderness few other frontiersmen ever knew.

This is what Pierre and I thought of when we talked our broken English, and when we were together ghosts of those days stalked the portages and phantom canoes moved down the lakes. On quiet nights it seemed we could hear the old *chansons* drifting across the water and hear the *voyageurs'* banter. I know when their story is weighed on the scales of history, the Pierres, Baptistes, and Jeans will be remembered not so much for what they did in the opening up of the continent, but for what they were. Theirs was a heritage of courage and spirit men will never forget.

Having seen most of the country within a radius of a few hundred miles of Ely, I longed to explore to the north and northwest as some of the older guides had done. Recalling their stories of the Albany, Sioux Lookout, and the Flin Flon, I knew the beautiful lake country of the Quetico-Superior was only a small part of the great route followed in the past. As years went by, it became my obsession to know the tremendous distances beyond, and to understand what motivated the *voyageurs* and the challenges that were theirs.

Though by the 1950's the country was finally mapped, with long-established Hudson's Bay posts scattered across it, the physical terrain was the same and vast reaches were as primitive as in the days of old.

Thus began a series of expeditions with friends who felt as I did. The famous Churchill River was the first, a thousand miles or more of lakes, rapids, and waterfalls extending from Île-à-la-Crosse in Saskatchewan to Hudson Bay. Though I had known the southern fringes of the Canadian Shield in the Quetico-Superior, I did not realize its real meaning and continental extent. We ran all the white water we could, lined where we dared not run, fought storms on the big lakes, and came to know the bush I had dreamed about for so long.

Once we followed the Camsell River north of the three-hundred-mile sweep of Great Slave Lake from the divide as far as Great Bear, with its cold, desolate barrens southwest of Coronation Gulf on the Arctic coast. From the west end we careened down the Bear River to the Mackenzie ninety miles away, and for the first time saw the route the famous explorer had followed in his search for the Northwest Passage, only to find its mouth in the ice floes of the Arctic Ocean.

We retraced the trail of David Thompson, beginning at Reindeer Lake, 160 miles to the mouth of the Swan, and finally went down the Fond du Lac to the Hudson's Bay post at Stony Rapids on Lake Athabasca, almost 300 miles from Fort Chipewyan at its far west end. This was the starting place of the famed Athabasca brigades who each year met those from Montreal at Grand Portage some 2000 miles away.

I saw the caribou migration on the Wolverine-Neganilini country northwest of Fort Churchill, came to know the open tundras beyond the limit of trees and the feel of the lonely barrens along the west coast of the Bay. Like the caribou, I sought shelter in the islands of dwarf spruce known as the taiga, the parklike stretches lying between the tundras and the treeline to the south. The land of little sticks, as it is called, taiga is a refuge for all living things, a sanctuary from blizzards of swirling whiteness, the long night, and the eternal cold.

We followed the Nelson, the Esquamish, and the Hayes down the historic route to Old York Factory on Hudson Bay, gazed as countless *voyageurs* had done over the blue and sparkling reaches of the sea itself, saw polar bears with their cubs, schools of white whales, and felt the frigid blasts from the ice pack in the straits above.

Later we saw the Ottawa, the Mattawa, and the French rivers, the beginning of the route from Montreal; heard the legends of Champlain and saw the portage where he lost his precious astrolabe in 1615. We portaged dangerous rapids on the French which had claimed the lives of many *voyageurs,* pictured the banks with their white crosses where in the high water of spring the great canoes were all but torn apart.

We passed through the narrow dalles all diarists wrote about with fear and delight, the places where parallel, rocky ridges make narrow canal-like chutes through which the canoes speed during times of flood. We did not run them, for this was fall and the waters were low, but as we portaged beside them we could almost hear the wild shouts as the thirty-five-foot Montreal canoes shot through, the banks close enough to touch. Then in the calm, placid area below, we looked as they had at the broad, blue expanses of Lake Huron with its hundreds of rocky, windswept islands and their tattered pines.

I saw the clear, green headwaters of the Yukon where it flows from the height of land above Skagway down through the fabled gold fields of 1898, and its brown and sluggish flow as it passes Fort Yukon on its way to the Bering Sea.

There were no rivers the traders failed to explore, no matter how distant or how remote. Some ventured so far they never did return, but wherever they went the goods went with them, packs that grew more valuable with every added mile from Montreal. The rapids cost lives, goods, and fur; every turbulent stretch of white water took its toll.

It was not until I stood again on the shore of Lake Superior at the site of old Grand Portage that the full significance and meaning of this vast land came home to me. Now I could see it all—the Quetico-Superior country, Lake of the Woods and Winnipeg, Saskatchewan and the Churchill. They lay before me now: Athabasca and Great Slave, the Mackenzie and Great Bear, the Nelson and the Hayes, the St. Lawrence, Ottawa, and French, the wide expanses of lakes Huron, Michigan, and Superior—the whole broad sweep of land and water that was theirs. What I saw was a living map of lakes, rivers, and forests, of mountains and plains, a map colored with disaster and disappointment, with challenge and triumph, with hopes and dreams. It took many years to understand the *voyageurs* and the lives they had led; seemed ages since I had guided with Pierre. I thought of him then and wondered if we would have been equal to the challenges that were theirs. I could hear him bellowing into the wind:

I'm proud of de sam' blood in my vein,
I'm a son of de Nort' Win' wance again—
So we'll fill her up till de bottle's drain,
An' drink to de Voyageur.

White Horses

The sunset over the little Indian settlement was startling. One of the last level rays caught the tip of the church spire and made it burst into flame for an instant. A faint chorus of dogs drifted to Tony and me across the water. It was a beautiful scene, but we were far too sleepy and tired to enjoy it for long.

It was dusk by the time we had stowed away the packs, checked the canoes and the outfit, covered everything, and weighted down ponchos and tarps with rocks, should the wind come up.

We crawled into our tents and into our sleeping-bags, lay there for a delicious moment before closing our eyes. Far off I thought I heard a dull roar. Perhaps it was the wind, or the Drum or Dipper or any one of the many rapids that were waiting for us in the morning.

I awakened once during the night and lay thinking of the approaching day and the warnings we had had. Running rapids in familiar country is one thing, running them in a strange land, where rock formations as well as the speed and depth of the water are different, is another.

While we were skirting the Shield and felt at home upon it, even so in the course of a thousand miles there was much to be learned. The Churchill was in flood. We had seen that at the dock, and when a river is high and out of bounds old landmarks mean nothing and there is always the danger of sweepers—windfalls with their scraggly tops reaching out like great brooms from newly eroded banks and catching anything that comes by. One bad move in white water and the expedition could end before it really got under way. We had asked about the rapids at Île-à-la-Crosse, had maps and notes from the Hudson's Bay Company as well as enlarged aerial photographs—all the data we could muster—but still we were not sure what to expect or what we would have to do.

The Indians traveling with their big canoes did not seem to understand what rivers could do to such little craft as ours and many of them for a generation or more had not been far from the posts. I remembered what one of them had said when he was questioned about a bad stretch of river.

"Oh, yes, I remember," he said. "My grandfather went there many years ago. 'Bad river,' he told us, 'very bad river.'"

All this went through my mind as I lay listening to the dull roar to the north. I knew the sound was worse at night and that the anticipation of any rapids that have never been seen can make an old canoeman blanch, if it is loud enough. The Drum was still miles away. Perhaps what I heard was the wind coming up and not the water at all. Still the roar persisted and then I knew it was not the wind, for there was no moaning in the jackpines back of the tent.

The morning dawned clear and calm and the east was red with the sunrise. But the sound was still there, rising and falling, sometimes almost inaudible. Everyone was conscious of it, although during breakfast there was no mention of what lay ahead.

The faint howl of a husky drifted to us as we slipped into the channel on our way to the river. Within half an hour the bay narrowed and now there was a perceptible movement of the water. The sound we had heard gradually became an all-engulfing roar. It submerged the rising wind, the swish of paddles, and the chuckles from the bow. As we moved into its center the old tight feeling within me grew, a feeling I have never overcome and possibly never will. Others may say they approach fast water with calm and assurance, but with me it is always the same. There was no escaping now, no turning back.

"White horses!" yelled Tony, and down below we could see the first of the silver spouts rising and falling. He had named them well back in the Quetico days. Now they were prancing before us again. The flow became swifter and swifter. Long streamers of water plants pointed straight ahead. There was no question of where to go—the current took care of that. The bank was in flood and the river raced through submerged clumps of willows and debris. This was dangerous, for we could not tell what lay underneath, with the old scoured-out channel nowhere to be seen.

The canoe raced ahead toward a melee of rocks with stumps and windfalls lodged against them. Denis reached far to the right, pulled the bow to one side, then to the left, and again to the right. Only he could see what lay ahead and as bowman his decisions were swift and final. The instant I saw him reach or swing the bow with a swift jerk of the paddle against the front gunwale, I followed with supporting action from the stern. We dodged from one tangle to another, each time slipping by smoothly without grazing obstructions.

So far all had gone well, and as we sped on our confidence grew. This was the easy part, according to the Indians—the place of fast water before the real rapids of the Drum began. As the speed increased, I began to wonder what it would be like below, how we could possibly find the portage in such a raging flood, and if we did find it in time, how we could check our plunge in time to land.

There was no choice now, no thinking back to what we might have done. We were committed. I glanced hurriedly over my right shoulder. Elliot and Eric in their customary bravado were shooting straight down the river. Expert canoemen with much white-water experience, their very nonchalance frightened me. Eric looked stern and competent; Elliot was laughing out loud.

Omond and Tony were slightly to their left, also heading down the center. That was wise, perhaps, as there the water would be deepest. Omond was an old hand and a veteran of many rivers. Tony knew more about polo ponies than canoes, but he had the balance, poise, and sensitivity of a ballet master. A good team, they would come through.

Our own canoe was hurtling down much closer to the bank, and Denis, who now placed his faith in the Good Saint of all *Voyageurs*, handled his paddle as though it were a spear, thrusting and feinting, pushing and pulling and at times even backing water to give me a chance to pull the craft around when the speed of the current made it seem as though we could not change our course. When he indicated a move, I backed him instantly with a thrust or twist of my own.

Now there were more rocks and swirls ahead, masses of floating willow brush with islands of muskeg torn from the bogs, all moving downstream in grand confusion. A final cluster of spouts, a last desperate surge to one side, and then we were milling around together in a big eddy down below, all breathless and excited with our first taste of the Churchill.

"Mon cher Bourgeois," said Denis, "we still have three canoes and we are all alive. We need put no crosses on the bank."

The real rapids of the Drum were below, with the portage supposedly on the left. At least that was the way it looked from where we sat. The legend on the Hudson's Bay Company map had said: "Natives shoot, others portage." That meant no shooting without knowing the rocks and ledges hidden beneath the flood.

We found the beginning of the portage shortly afterward, threw on the packs and canoes, and sloshed along through a swamp, over rocks, and around new windfalls carried down by the river. It seemed good to be there on the ground no matter what the condition of the trail, for now the roar was deafening and the white horses spouting high and wild. At the end of the portage we loaded the canoes again and coasted a churning millrace for half a mile before we left the Drum.

Leaf Rapids was now ahead, and here the legend said: "Portage just above and to the left, but can be shot by good canoemen and with care." Care was underlined. That meant us, with our prowess with canoes and ability to read water that was in flood or messed up with floating vegetation. I was in the lead, the other canoes now holding back to see what I would do. As I drew close, the spouts below looked desperate. So thick were they it was impossible to see any sort of channel between them. We skirted the drop and shot toward the left bank, and when close to the shore turned into a narrow V because of the growing swiftness of the current.

No sooner had we started down than the canoe leaped into the air and there was a sharp, sickening crack. To an old canoeman this is the most frightening sound in the world, for it means that you have hit a rock head on. But there was no time for reflection or even fear. In an instant we were off the ledge, dodging rocks and debris. No water was spurting in, which meant the canvas was still sound.

The other men, having seen what happened to us, took a channel still farther out and our three canoes moved down the river, zigzagging between boulders and spouting rocks. Swifter and swifter went the canoes, picking V's of smooth water and avoiding white horses and waves. There was good going ahead. Now we were a team, the stern paddle sensing what the bow would do, responding to every movement no matter how slight. Near the end was a rough-looking barricade with no apparent opening. We approached cautiously, and just as we had decided not to take a chance but head for the bank, Denis noticed a rift just big enough to take us, with a smooth slick running beyond. Instantly we turned, and with a swoosh shot through the opening. Then we were at the bottom with the others milling around in the foam-laced whirlpools, all of us looking back in half-frightened amazement at the wild staircase down which we had come.

Each canoe had suffered slight damage, but we were proud that we had come through as well as we did. "That was fun," said Elliot, as he mopped up the water in the bottom of his canoe.

Omond had hauled out his map and was studying it carefully. I paddled over and Denis took hold of his gunwale.

"Deer Rapids coming up," he said. "'No portage here,' says the legend, 'but can be shot by good canoemen or *voyageurs*.'"

"Well," said Eric, "what do you think, Bourgeois?"

I shrugged my shoulders. "Let's wait and see."

By now we were skeptical of all advice. If no portage was marked, the rapids were usually run. We would look it over, pick a route as we had done before, and shoot. This was not an easy thing to do with the river high, we had discovered, for channels ran off through the trees and over obstructions that were not marked on the maps or in the experience of those who had gone down during periods of normal flow. It became increasingly difficult to tell where the real river bank began. Whatever we did would have to depend on how the water looked when we approached the drop.

Outcroppings of the Shield had disappeared again and the shores were swampy and low. This was why the river seemed to be running all over the woods. Deer Rapids was evidently far away, for we could hear nothing and could see no spouts in the distance. We soon forgot its threat while watching the growing number of terns and gulls wheeling and screaming above us. For a time we forgot that Deer would have to be run before we could make our camp that night.

The river now was fairly alive with birds. It seemed at times as though there were thousands in the air, wheeling and dipping, and screaming constantly. I had the feeling that they too were part of the flood, that they and the land, the water, and the air were all moving along together. So strong did this sense of fluidity become that the canoes themselves seemed part of the river with the soaring and flashing of wings above it.

This was a great breeding ground for ducks; many mallards, redheads, and scaup rose from each little backwater or eddy. The whisper of their wings blended with the screaming of terns until we scarcely noticed another sound coming in: the steady background music of another rapids in the distance.

If the rapids were really bad, there would have been a portage marked somewhere in the records. So I comforted myself as we made the approach to Deer. Soon the sound grew louder, and by standing up I could see the first of the white horses. We drifted as close as we dared to the brink, spotted what looked like a good channel with a wide-open V at its throat and headed down its center. The V continued smooth and black, connected with other V's, and down went all three canoes in line. This was good water to run, with plenty of depth for once and plenty of warning, too, the tail of each V marked plainly by a spout. Down we sped with an abandon we had not known before, and the farther we went the more confident we became. This was a rapids we could enjoy. Then, as before, we were in a whirlpool at its base. Not a rock had we touched, nor a drop of water shipped. We had come down as canoemen should.

Deer Rapids had been good for our morale. We knew about the rocks now, the color of the Churchill, its speed and depth, the sweepers along the banks. We had survived several runs and our record had been clean, with the exception of Leaf. Perhaps what had happened there was just as well, for it had given us a hint of what could happen if we relaxed our vigilance or went down without proper reconnaissance. We needed the memory of Leaf.

One more rapids lay ahead, one final challenge before we could camp. The map said of Dipper: "Portage all the time."

There were no decisions to make; we had only to find the trail. I knew Indians never carried a foot farther than they had to. If they could approach within a hairbreadth of the lip of a chute, they would, rather than land fifty or a hundred feet above, where it was perfectly safe. I also remembered the old adage "No Indian ever drowned on a portage." But with the river the way it was, finding a portage under a swirling torrent presented a problem.

As we neared the rapids the flow became swifter and swifter and higher over the banks, and we were soon convinced that this time the portage was under water. While we were debating whether to slip into the willows or go down a little farther, I saw an old blaze on a jackpine marking the carry, but the water there was several feet deep. Portaging was out of the question, and by the looks of the heavy rapids down below shooting was impossible as well. Just above the jackpine, Denis and I jumped into the water, pulled our canoe into the willows, and worked our way gradually downstream around windfalls and almost impenetrable thickets, holding on as best we could to keep from dropping completely out of sight between the boulders.

Elliot and Eric, Omond and Tony pushed inland toward drier ground; Denis and I paralleled the river farther down. Eventually we found a brush-choked ancient trail, evidence of high water many years before, and made the carry to the other end. Through the trees and heavy brush we could see the white horses, great herds of them galloping in wild confusion all over the river. No canoes could live out there and we were glad to be on solid ground.

After the rapids, the marshy expanses of Dipper Lake were a relief as the river fanned out into a great delta with grassy flats and winding channels. Once more there was screaming above us, while the shorebirds and waders ran over tangled weed mats, and the pelicans coasted the horizon like little white ships. The sun shone on countless wings, and the sound of calling was everywhere.

Across the marshes were cliffs and rocky islands, and we would camp once more on the Shield. There were several places to choose from with ledges and glaciated shelves all along the shore. We decided on a sheltered island just across the channel from a cluster of Indian cabins on the mainland. High enough to catch the full sweep of the sunset, we would get its color over the marshes and be within sound of the moving flocks. As we neared, we saw again the same orange lichens that marked our first campsite and a smooth landing place close to the water's edge. It felt good to unload the canoes that night and from our vantage point look over the country through which we had come. We stood there high above it and remembered the Drum, Leaf, Deer, and Dipper rapids. I thought of Dr. Charles Camsell, the great geologist and explorer, reminiscing on his days in the Canadian bush. "Of course I've known fear," he said, "but always fear laced with exhilaration."

That day, with white horses all the way from Shagwenaw, we had known fear too, and also the joy that comes when a run is over and you sit in some foam-laced eddy at a rapids' base, looking back. No one who has ever done that can forget the sight, the sound, and the feel of fast water or the wonder and sense of triumph.

The Falls

The portage around Trout Lake Falls was a pretty one skirting the brink and ending just below where the water was a-churn and covered with foam and the air full of the sound of it.

Out in the open again, we turned in our canoe, sat there in the swirling currents feasting our eyes and senses, then just across the channel found a campsite on a smooth, rocky shelf above a roaring rapids, the sound of it merging with the music of the falls.

The river swirled deeply off the ledge, and I asked Tony and Elliot to get some fish for supper as soon as the tents were up and the outfit safely put away. Later, Omond joined them and the first strike was his. A tremendous pike broke water—all of three feet in length and broad across the back. It fought in the current, coming to the surface time and again, then bore down into the depths and headed out into the open river only to come charging back toward the landing.

While watching, I heard a shout from Elliot: "I've got a monster too!" And sure enough, not twenty feet away he was fighting another just as large. He ran down the shore to get away from Omond's line, the two of them far too involved to notice that Tony just above them was in the same predicament, also having hooked one of the huge great northerns for which this country is famous. All camp activity came to a stop as we watched three fish being landed at the same time, each determined to break tackle in the swift current of the river.

Omond's came in first, a pike over twenty pounds, then within minutes Elliot's, and finally Tony's. We laid the three fish on the rocks. They totaled sixty-odd pounds. We admired them, delivered the coup de grace with a beaver stick waiting by the fireplace, then wondered what to do with our prizes. It was too late for pictures and too much to eat at one time, so I decided to clean them at once, use what we could for supper and breakfast, and smoke the rest to carry along for lunch snacks during the next few days.

What beautiful fillets they were—golden yellow in color, about twenty-four inches in length, four inches wide, and an inch to an inch and a half in thickness. The frying pan was waiting, and after rolling two of the steaks in flour, I dropped them into the hot bacon fat. Elliot mixed a batch of mashed potatoes, and we ate until we could hold no more.

With what was left of the fried fillets, I stirred up enough fish cakes for breakfast, using the old recipe of fish, mashed potatoes, dehydrated onions, a dash of flour to hold them together, and some powdered egg for color and flavoring. Twelve cakes were placed in a pan to wait for dawn.

Then I went to work on the remaining four fillets, cleaned them thoroughly, rubbed them down with salt, pepper, and bacon fat, and laid them on the grate over a smoldering fire made of peeled sticks from an old beaver house. No spruce or pine went into the smoking fire, only the cleanest of birch or aspen, thoroughly dried and cured. The fillets quickly turned to a golden brown and I tended them carefully, knowing that for days ahead we would have something other than sausage and cheese for lunch.

We could have caught a dozen pike had we wished, for the waters between the falls and the rapids were alive with minnows. I am sure we could have taken several hundred pounds. The three we had taken were large, but I knew they could be even larger. One recorded in the Quetico region was well over forty pounds. Samuel Hearne in his early journal mentioned the size of the pike. "Pike," he said, "also grow to an incredible size in this water, and I have seen some that weighed upwards of forty pounds."

Long after my friends had rolled in, I sat before the fire tending the big steaks. It was a satisfying task. The preparation of food is always satisfying on the trail. I nibbled the edge of one of them, salted them again slightly and basted them with bacon grease. Trout ordinarily need no basting, for they are fat in themselves, but these fillets of the big northern pike, or jackfish as they are called all over Canada, are proverbially lean and dry.

The night was clear, the stars bright, no bird calls, no loons or huskies, no sound but the rushing of water. Around me the great silence once more. It was good to sit there watching the slow fire and listen. This was still the old north, the Lonely Land, but I wondered how long it would remain so, with Canada's industrial expansion on the way and the burgeoning population increase, not only in the United States but within Canada itself.

This was the soft underbelly of the last great wilderness on the continent. I could see civilization to the south lying against it like a hungry young animal probing, pushing, exploring, milking the untouched resources above, and as it fed, making its growth felt. Bursting with vitality, it must gorge itself on the sustenance there for the taking. Already there was talk of a road from Lac la Ronge, another to Île-à-la-Crosse, and one to Athabasca to tap the unexploited country to the north and the oil and the minerals with which it is blessed.

Wilderness had come to be a precious thing to us and to many thousands, and I wondered how it would be if people no longer had any knowledge of wild country or any opportunity to know what *voyageurs* had known.

The falls were fading now in the dusk, but I could hear

them more plainly than ever, music that had not changed in thousands of years. Then it seemed as if there was a different note, a certain somberness that had not been there before. As I listened, I could hear still another sound, an obligato to the rest, an exuberance and a pulsing-with-life as there always is on the frontiers of the world.

I turned the steaks once more. They were all an even, golden brown now and their flavor about right. I put on a few more small sticks, banked them with ashes so they would not flame, moved the grate a little higher, then went into the tent. As I lay in my bag I could hear the singing of the rapids with the deep roar of the falls as a steady undertone, and I lay there half asleep listening to a symphony with many shades of meaning.

According to Omond, we were 208 miles along our course —almost halfway to our goal. Ahead was the Lake of the Dead. I wondered about it and the story that would surely come when Eric read from David Thompson's diary again. It was hard to imagine any great tragedy in such a peaceful land, but I knew what disease could do to native tribes, as well as starvation and bitter winters when gales howled out of the Arctic and the mercury dropped to fifty or sixty below zero. These summer months were easy ones on the Churchill.

There was a flicker of light from the fireplace. Evidently one of the sticks of aspen was burning too brightly. I went out of the tent and covered the wood with ashes once more. Tony waked and joined me, and we sat in the soft glow of the embers.

"It has been a good day," he said. "One of the best. And wasn't that something having three pike on at the same time? You know, some nights I almost hate to go to sleep for fear I shall miss something, so when I found you were not in your bag, I came out."

I cut off a sliver of the smoked fish, handed it to him, and he sat munching it before the fire. He smacked his lips. "Better than smoked sturgeon," he said. "Better than caviar from the Caspian."

I cut off another sliver for myself, and it was very good. We had about ten or twelve pounds to carry with us and could have smoked enough to last us the rest of the trip, but there would be fish everywhere and a fresh smoking was always best.

Before we went back into the tent, I once more stoked the fire very carefully. We carried the three great heads and the skins and entrails to a little point of rock just below camp. Gulls would find them in the morning and clean up swiftly. Their calling and screaming would wake us at dawn.

The first rays of the sun came over the far ridge and touched the top of the falls. The plunging spray sparkled with light. The light shone on the sea of mist over the river, and its whiteness boiled and fumed. The valley was full of the sound of rushing water. A flock of mallards whispered by overhead on their way to some feeding ground above Trout Portage.

I loosened the ax from where I had left it in a log and walked over to a dead tree that had some good, dry branches. When I raised the ax I became more conscious than ever of the quiet, and I could not bear the thought of what a shattering blow would do. The *voyageurs* should sleep another half-hour. Nothing must disturb the spell that lay over the river. I walked back to the fireplace, laid down the ax, gathered an armful of squaw wood, sticks, a handful of pine needles, and shreds of bark from the ground to start a fire. When the tinder burst into flame, I carefully laid the wood on, went to the water's edge, filled the pots and put them to boil.

The falls were blazing now and the sun was burning the mist off the rapids. By the time breakfast was ready, the river would be clear.

The smoked fish was done, the long brown fillets cold and stiff. I cut off a fine sliver and munched it with satisfaction as I nursed the fire. The fish was good and salted just right. I hung the fillets in a bush nearby where they might catch a little more of the smoke before being packed away.

A pinch of salt went into the porridge pot. As the water came to a rolling boil, I added two cupfuls of raisins, and the meal, then put the pot at the edge of the grate, where it would simmer until done, and the pail of boiling coffee in the ashes to steep.

"Good morning," said Tony.

I was startled. So engrossed was I with the cooking, the scene before me, and the little tasks of getting breakfast ready, I had not heard him stir or come out of the tent.

"What a spot we have found," he said. "And such fishing." He went over to the fillets and stroked their long smooth surfaces fondly.

I poured a cup of coffee for him and gave him a slice of smoked pike.

He sat down beside the fire and stared into the flames.

"Where to, today?" he asked.

"Lake of the Dead," I replied, "unless the wind stops us."

"Lake of the Dead," he repeated, and took a bite of smoked pike. "What a bad name in such beautiful country."

I recalled Mackenzie's diary and the explanation he had given.

"But that was long ago," he said, "and the Indians have come back. What worries me now is this talk of roads and the opening up of all this country."

"I've been thinking of that too," I answered. It reminded me of what Hemingway had said in *Green Hills of Africa*:

A continent ages quickly once we come. The natives live in harmony with it. But the foreigner destroys, cuts down the trees, drains the water, so that the water supply is altered and in a short time the soil, once the sod is turned under, is cropped out and, next, it starts to blow away as it has blown away in every old country and as I had seen it start to blow in Canada. The earth gets tired of being exploited. A country wears out quickly unless man puts back in it all his residue and that of all his beasts. When he quits using beasts and uses machines, the earth defeats him quickly. The machine can't reproduce, nor does it fertilize the soil, and it eats what he cannot raise. A country was made to be as we found it. We are the intruders and after we are dead we may have ruined it but it will still be there and we don't know what the next changes are. I suppose they all end up like Mongolia.

The mist was gone from the river now and the rapids

sparkled and sang in the sunlight. They were still young as the land was young, and the great machines seemed far away. All that counted now were the rapids ahead, seven stretches of white water to test our skill. This day belonged to adventurers.

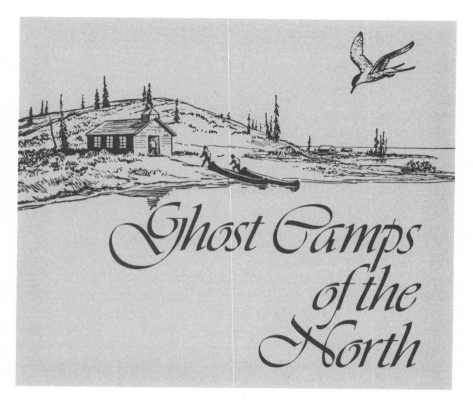

Ghost Camps of the North

The *voyageurs* of our expedition had battled their way up the Camsell River from the height of land above Great Slave toward the barren bleakness of Great Bear. It was a time of rain and cold; the winds off the Arctic ice never ceased. The terrain had grown more and more rugged, and each day we fought the waves, dodged behind islands, and skirted dangerous promontories we could not avoid. We ran what rapids our canoes could take, but when they were bad we portaged—in that icy water we dared not take a chance.

The hills were almost mountainous now, great glaciated masses of rock, the ragged growth of spruce all but gone except along the lake shores and in the valleys of connecting streams. It was a savage land and full of beauty, even where the fires had been and billowing ridges of granite lay bare to pitiless gales.

Not a soul had we seen since our trip began, no Indians or vestiges of their camps. They had migrated long ago to the milder climate of the Mackenzie Valley to the west. There was more game to hunt, riverboats and barges passed constantly on their way to Norman Wells and Aklavik, and activity was never lacking around the Hudson's Bay posts and the missions. The Camsell lay deserted as though the glacier had just retreated. So accustomed had we been to seeing no one, it was with great excitement we saw something strange on the opposite shore of a lake on the way to Hottah.

We got out the glasses and studied it intently. It was a wrecked plane, a DC-3 lying at a crazy angle against the bank, with one wing much lower than the other, behind it several cabins, possibly a mine or some trader's outfit. Quickly we changed course and headed toward it. That low wing meant trouble, and in the north a downed plane is never ignored. As we neared, we studied it again. There was no mistake, the craft was lying close against the rocky shore.

We pushed swiftly now and on the way passed a little island, its bare surface completely covered with a mat of orange lichen. I could not resist taking a color shot as we passed—a spot of orange with tufts of golden grass against the leaden background of the lake. We landed at what had once been a dock. The planks were broken now, the piling loose and tilted. The aircraft was only a shell, one motor gone, the other a wreck, the interior stripped and dismantled. The loading door hung on its hinges and creaked in the wind. The tipped wing was supported by a crib of logs. There was nothing to salvage; it would stay there for a long time, gleaming against the shore. We walked up the well-beaten trail to one of the cabins, opened the unlocked door, and stepped inside.

This was the cook shack, the table set for twenty men. Bread and butter were still there, meat, mashed potatoes, jelly and jam. A pumpkin pie with one wedge missing stood at the end. The gravy bowl was full, the sliced bread and cake hard. Nothing had been touched or molested; there were no signs of squirrels, mice, or rats, no decay or spoilage. It was as though the men had left just the day before in the middle of a meal.

I went into the kitchen. Its shelves were stocked with food, hundreds of dollars' worth, enough to keep the crew going for months, tinned supplies precious in this far country, vegetables, strawberries, peaches, meats, and sausage. In a back lean-to hung a dried-up haunch of moose, a hide, and a slab of bacon. Shining utensils hung on the walls: pots and pans, knives, skillets, spoons. Nothing was out of place.

We left and walked into the next building, the office of the engineer and superintendent. On a drafting table was an unfinished sketch of the mining property, a file for letters and plans. I thumbed through the file; the last letter was dated at the close of the Korean war—six years before. A uranium mine, it had been discontinued when rich prospects close to civilization no longer warranted its operation. A mahogany box contained a new theodolite in a velvet case. It had never been used and was worth a great deal of money. Surveying instruments stood in a corner; drill bits and flat iron strips and bars were laid neatly on separate racks.

The men's quarters and bunkhouses were the same—items of personal equipment, gloves, shirts, rain gear, and boots all left behind in the hurry of departure. On a small table beside one of the bunks I picked up a cluster of quartz crystals. Some were stained with iron, some the color of old rose, others close to amethyst. They were clear and well shaped. On one crystal was a deposit of silver, between two other faces was a tiny speck of the same orange lichen we had seen on the little island while crossing the lake. Since it was a perfect specimen, I picked it up, dropped it into my pocket. It is before me now as I write, and brings the scene of that abandoned mining camp back to me.

We returned to the cook shack, sat down at the table with the uneasy feeling that the men who had been there last were still around, the cook busying himself in the kitchen before his stove, the cookee bringing in the food, seeing the gravy was hot, the teapot full. None of us spoke. This was a place of ghosts. Ten years, or a hundred, it would make little difference in that frigid climate. We closed the door carefully so no animals would get in.

Back in the engineer's office, we picked up the theodolite and placed it carefully in one of the half-empty packs. It was very heavy, but none of us could bear the thought of leaving it behind. We would drop it off eventually at Eldorado on Great Bear.

We took some tinned fruit and meat, went back to the canoes, pushed off toward the lichen-covered rock and east toward our rendezvous on Great Bear. As we rounded the last point, I turned and looked back. There was the gleam of silver, behind it the dark cluster of cabins, the table still set, the engineer's shack, the bunkhouses, the hopes and dreams of men who had lived and perhaps died there. Too costly to fly out, the camp was left as many others were in the far reaches of the north. Some day, should the demand warrant, it might open again, but now it was better lost and forgotten.

Not until we reached Eldorado did we learn the story — how one of the supply planes had gone through the crust of spring ice and hurtled into the bank. One wing had been almost sheared, an engine ruined, the fuselage twisted out of shape — no casualties, just one of those accidents that happen to bush pilots all over the north. The men had saved what they could, but there the wreck would stay until the elements corroded the aluminum and it finally sank into the water and muck along the shore.

Two years later I came across another ghost camp almost a thousand miles to the southeast. It was during the course of a caribou survey where the endless tundra bordering Hudson Bay meets the scraggly line of the taiga, that land of stunted spruce, muskeg, and caribou moss that extends not only through our own north but across all of Siberia as well. The migration was on, and we were flying in to join a research party tagging the caribou in an attempt to determine how they moved.

From the air, Duck Lake Post of the Hudson's Bay Company looked like any other on the tundra, or for that matter anywhere in the north: a white building with a red roof, a cluster of storage sheds and shacks, a warehouse for furs and supplies, canoe racks, a little dock. Built on a bare point of land between Duck Lake and Nejanilini, it once served the scattered bands of Swampy Crees and even some of the Eskimo of the Wolverine–Seal River country, as far west as Nueltin and east to Hudson Bay. It was isolated enough so that travelers seldom came and, when they did, it was a momentous event.

But this time there was no running about, no waving or frantic preparations for our arrival, no smoke from the chimneys, no tents or shelters around the post or canoes pulled up on the shore, no dogs straining at their chains and howling their hearts out in the excitement of our landing. Not a soul was to be seen anywhere, only a lone fox streaking across the point for the cover of the willow fringe beyond. We swung low to be sure of the approach, buzzed the little gray deserted church across the bay. It was weather-beaten, with the windows gone and grass growing around its steps. The cross was at an angle leaning away from the wind.

We landed a quarter-mile out in the lake, taxied cautiously to the dock. The outer cribbing was broken by the ice, the planking torn apart. We had difficulty in warping the *Norseman* into position because of sharp, protruding rocks, but finally tied it fast and walked up the trail to the main building. The Hudson's Bay Company sign was gone, and there was nothing to indicate ownership. The store was still in good repair but the shelves were empty. I went into the kitchen and started a fire in the stove. It smoked at first, but after the debris and soot burned out it drew well. The coffee pot, kettles, and skillets were clean and we used them rather than get out our own. Supper was served in the small dining room where the factor had eaten many times with guests who came to visit. Beds and bunks were still in place in the attic. Some of us bedded down there.

I decided to sleep in the warehouse beside the old fur press. I wanted to be alone there to catch, perhaps, the feeling of the days when Duck Lake Post was alive. It was dark when I went over, and the great door complained when I put my shoulder against it and pushed it in. I lit a stub of a candle and placed it on a shelf, laid out my bag in the center and close to the open door, lay there in the flickering candlelight surveying my abode. To one side was a beaten-up freighter canoe long unused, on the other the press — a huge one with a great screw turned by an iron bar. Into that press had gone the fur to be made up into bales for the trip down the Wolverine to South Indian, or down the Seal to the Bay. Along the walls were shelves for storage and rows of hooks for hides. I could see it in the spring after the fur was in, foxes and wolves, muskrats and beaver, wolverine, mink, and otter. I could smell it, too, for even though the hides were long gone, their pungence remained, an almost fetid and musky smell, a combination of all the creatures trapped in the north. Here, years before, lay the wealth of the region, the result of uncounted days and months of labor, privation, and danger. It had once held food and traps and equipment for all the surrounding native bands. This was more than a warehouse for fur and supplies, it was a bastion of security for all who lived within range.

I blew out the candle finally and went to sleep. Not a sound disturbed me all night long — no howling of huskies, no scurrying of mice or squirrels. I wakened once and listened, but there was only the lap of the waves down at the shore. The night was cloudy and dark, and though I had braced the door with a stout log, it creaked in the rising wind.

In the morning to my joy the sun was out and I went onto the ramp to dress and to lace my boots. The planks were hand-hewn, shaped with ax and knife and rasp and held together with wooden dowel pins. That approach to the great door was made to last. Up it had come bales and boxes from the canoes and boats and sleds, and down had gone the pressed bales of fur. I threw on my parka, went down to the shore and washed in the icy water, then walked down the length of the peninsula. The stakes that had marked the tents were still in place and, with them, the debris of all Indian camps: shreds of cloth, worn moccasins, torn rubbers, the whitened, well-gnawed bones of caribou. It seemed to me I could almost hear the Indians talking, could smell their fires, sense the coming and going.

The country, too, seemed as though it had reverted to its ancient self now that it was abandoned. The barren tundra stretched endlessly in all directions, and marching up the hills were the scattered spruce of the taiga, in which the caribou sought shelter from winter storms. The lake sparkled in the sunshine as it had for thousands of years; the land itself was as beautiful and full of meaning and challenge as it had ever been. Something was gone, however, a certain something that had been there before. It was Duck Lake Post that had changed with its abandonment.

I stood at the far end of the spit looking back toward the post with its rising plume of smoke, picturing it as it used to be when the smoke of many fires hung like a haze over the entire point. Greetings, goodbyes, tales of high adventure, sadness and joy—all these were gone.

I knew then that though one loves a land, one still needs the warmth of companionship with others of his kind and must not always travel alone. I had ghost camps of my own and country haunted with memories of those who had been with me. One of these places was a little campsite at the mouth of the Range River, where it empties into Low Lake in the Quetico-Superior country. No one but my partner Dean and I had ever used this spot, for from the water's edge it looked like a marshy flat; but, actually, beyond the fringe of alders it was high and dry, with the shelf of grass sheltered well by a broadly branching jackpine. Here we laid our sleeping-bags and gear when the bluebill flight was on, and for many years knew such companionship as only those can who share some common joy.

The place for the fire was close to a shelf of gray rock in back of the pine, and at night, if we were lucky, the light shone on the blue and green of wingbars and the branches of the jackpine were a tracery of black above us. We stored our food in a crevice of the rock and always tucked away some kindling for a quick fire there. The river wound behind us, an open road to the Range Lake country and the border, while to the south and west were the golden rice beds, with a stand of tall pines against the sunset. We placed decoys in the mouth of the river, for sooner or later something always came by. I will never forget the breathtaking roar of a bunch of bluebills coming down the river, the canvas-ripping sound of them as they dipped. Sometimes mallards lifted out of the rice and headed up river. Jacksnipe always began the day with their cheeping, and after dawn flocks of snowbirds drifted across the mud flats bordering the channel.

For many years Dean and I used the place, and we came to love its sights and sounds and smells and the joy of all these things together, but then one day he took the trail to another hunting ground and our joy was gone. For a while I went back alone as though he were still with me, and I could hear his banter then and see him moving around as he had before. When I lay in my sleeping-bag on the grassy shelf, I was conscious of the depression beside me, and when a flock came over high I could hear him whisper, "Listen—there'll be action in the morning."

After a time I no longer returned to my ghost camp. It was better, I thought, to keep it with memories that were mine alone. For me that little camp had become a place of dreams. Others may go there now and perhaps they are finding what I found and building associations of their own. And so it is with all country. While the meaning of wilderness never changes to those who understand it, it means even more if you have sunk your roots in deeply. No country can ever be bleak or forbidding if it has once been a part of the love and warmth of those who have shared it with you.

Whenever I travel the lake and river country of the north, I meet friends of other days. They are with me constantly on campsites and portages, and I hear them everywhere. Never again will I travel the Rainy, the Churchill, the Camsell, the Bear, the Burntwood, or any other routes without reliving adventures with companions who have been with me. The terrain has a different meaning, not only through what we shared, but because of what we knew that gave us the feeling of the land itself: its eras of the past, the time when the Canadian Shield came into being, when prehistoric seas laid down formations of Athabasca sandstone, the glacial periods of the last million years when the routes we traveled were shaped by the gouging of the ice, the crossing of Asiatics over Bering Strait and their slow filtration into the south, the days of explorers and *voyageurs*, up to the swiftly changing time of today. All this we had shared and lived over many thousands of miles, until almost unconsciously the long history of the primitive country we had traversed was absorbed into our minds and thoughts. We had left no mark on the country itself, but the land had left its mark on us. . . .

The smoke was still rising high from the kitchen of the old post. Breakfast must be ready, I thought, and hurried back. The wind was coming up and we still had far to go.

Painted Rocks

Indian paintings are found on smooth cliff faces all over the Quetico-Superior area. Reddish brown in color and seldom large, they adorn the rocks along many major routes of travel as high as a man can reach from a canoe. These strange likenesses of animals and birds, of suns and moons, canoes and figures of symbolic meaning are found from the Atlantic to the Pacific, as well as along the waterways of the Canadian Shield.

No one today knows when they were done, who the artists were, or what they mean. All we know is that the pigment used was a combination of fish oil or animal fat with one of the iron oxides common to the continent; and that they are similar not only to the petroglyphs, or rock carvings, of our west but to the prehistoric paintings and carvings in many other countries of the world. We can only wonder about their meaning, but believe that, whatever they portray and wherever they are, they represent the first groping attempts of Stone Age man for the expression of his creative powers.

To realize the possibility that some of these pictographs might be close to Listening Point was exciting. One morning, when the water was sparkling and a tail wind holding from the west, my wife, Elizabeth, and I paddled to the place where we had heard they might be found. For years I had wanted to locate them, but had always gone off on longer expeditions to the north.

The shoreline toward the east was rugged, seemed to have few of the vertical cliffs of smooth rock faces rising from the water's edge where we had always found them before. Just as we were about to give up our search, we slipped in close to a high, bush-covered slope and discovered there an open face of ledge hidden behind a clump of trees. Hopefully we pushed aside the branches, expecting the familiar figures, but all we saw was some iron staining partly obscured by lichen. Though we examined the entire cliff carefully, exploring every possibility, we found nothing even remotely resembling a pictograph. While we sat there in a canoe wondering where the paintings might be, a swift vision of those we had found in other places passed before me.

A month earlier I had been at the famous pictured rocks of Crooked Lake along the border, where the cliffs rise straight and sheer for a hundred feet or more. The rocks themselves are very beautiful there, colored by lichens and stained in long, undulating ribbons of color by the iron formations above. The bands are gray and orange and black, with patterns of blues and greens, and when the water ripples, reflections of these ribbons of color extend below in a shimmering liquid curtain as though the cliffs had fanned out onto the surface. But even though the unusual beauty of the cliffs themselves has stopped travelers for centuries, it is the smooth face protected by an overhanging ledge that is of the most interest today. Here some forgotten race recorded in magic symbols its deeds of prowess and valor. Here are moose, pelicans, war canoes, a loon with a fish inside, a medicine man with horns on his head, a caribou that looks like an ibex from the Asiatic mainland.

One of the famous landmarks along the *voyageurs'* highway and known to thousands of travelers in the days of the fur trade, the paintings were never mentioned in traders' journals. Explorers spoke of the colors of the cliff and called it the Rock of Arrows because at one time the great crack which cuts diagonally across it was full of feathered shafts. The cliff was a meeting place for *voyageurs* from Lake Superior on their way to the far northwest and those who were returning from Athabasca and the Mackenzie.

Alexander Henry the Younger mentioned the rock in one of his journals in 1800: "Thence we went down several ugly rapids . . . portaged 100 paces over a rock to Lac la Croch. At the Rock of Arrows, we met nine canoes loaded with Athabasca packs. At sunset we came to Portage de Rideau [Curtain Falls] where we stopped for the night."

But not a word about the Indian paintings on the cliffs, only mention of the war party and rendezvous with other expeditions. If they had only known that the Indian paintings were of far greater significance, their diaries would have been full of awe and wonderment. We can only conclude that pictographs were so common along their entire route of travel from Montreal that they were not considered important enough to be mentioned. It has been suggested they might have been done after the days of the fur trade were past, but if that were so, modern Indians would surely understand their meaning and know what tribes had done them.

The area surrounding the Point is rich in such paintings. To the north, in a bay of Darkey Lake, are some of the finest, so clear and sharp and unfaded they might have been made in recent times. I paddled by them not long ago and was horrified to find a fringe of protecting birch gone and the paintings fully exposed to the sun for the first time in my memory. Beavers were the vandals, had cut the trees for food and had stored the topmost branches in the water around a newly built lodge near by. These paintings show a hunting expedition, a moose cow and calf with footprints on either side, a great sea serpent with a horned head surrounded by hunters in canoes.

On Hegman Lake a few miles to the northeast is another splendid group showing a bull moose with wide-branching antlers, as well done as though a modern artist had conceived it. A pelican stands to one side and on the other a mountain lion with a long, curving tail.

To the north, on Lac la Croix, are cliffs where men of the past dipped their hands into pigment and pressed them against the wall. Some of the imprints are very large, others childlike in size. Such hand-paintings also occur in the caves of the Dordogne in France and in Spain. The privilege of leaving such a mark may have been a reward for valor or a pledge of loyalty. No one will ever know.

Paintings are found on the Kawishiwi and Isabella rivers to the south, and no doubt hidden surfaces will be discovered for years to come as the country becomes better known.

On an expedition down the Churchill River in upper Manitoba and Saskatchewan, I found them all along the route of travel. Though they were a thousand miles or more to the northwest of the Quetico-Superior, in the land of the Woodland Crees, they were identical to the rest. But in addition, there was a type of figure I had seen nowhere else and one whose meanings some of the older Indians still understood. These were the Maymaygwayshi, who, according to legend, are little people with round heads and no noses who live with only one purpose: to play jokes on travelers. The tiny creatures have long spidery legs, arms with six-fingered hands, and live between rocks in the rapids. When a canoe comes hurtling down, their greatest delight is to grasp the ends of paddles, and if the craft tips over, their shrieks of joy can be heard above the thunder of the water. If anything strange or unaccountable happens anywhere in the land of the Crees, it is the Maymaygwayshi who are responsible.

And here at last were Indians who knew something of the meaning of the rock paintings. Though none knew who did them and many scoffed at their authenticity, the story of the

Maymaygwayshi had survived. At one portage, until recent times, Indians still left offerings of food, tobacco, or trinkets at a rock where the little people were painted in order to ensure safe passage through the rapids below. If these small figures meant something to the Crees, others must have had significance as well.

Here again, along the far reaches of the Churchill, was evidence of the creative impulse in Stone Age man that had produced the pictographs not only on this continent but all over the world. Though colors might vary, they were generally composed of mixtures of the different oxides of iron with animal fats—yellow from the ocher, black from the manganese, reds and browns from limonites and hematites. Iron-bearing rock is a common mineral, and when powdered and mixed with any fat it becomes a durable pigment that, where protected from the elements, can survive for centuries with little change in brilliance.

Through such primitive painting it has been possible to trace the development of man's attempt to portray not only the life around him but his dreams and fears. From the first scratchings on the rock walls of caves to rude outlines of forms and the final artistic and colorful figures of animals with which he was familiar we see the story of his progress. Even more significant than the beauty and perfection of these ancient paintings of the Stone Age was the emergence' thousands of years before the oldest civilizations of the use of line and suggestion to portray the world of magic and spirit and hidden meaning.

According to prehistorians, some thirty thousand years passed before the primitive markings on walls of rock developed into naturalistic painting. Another twenty thousand years later appeared the first attempts at expressionism, and only during the last five thousand, the hieroglyphic symbols that preceded the written alphabets of Western civilization.

The pictographs I had found along the canoe routes to the north were as important as any in the world. Their actual age did not matter. They may have been done only a few centuries ago or belong to the post-Ice Age. Whatever their final designation in the research of moderns, we know that, together with all the other surviving examples of prehistoric art, they are among the most ancient records of mankind, tell of the eons when man pondered his environment while the awareness slowly came upon him that the dark mysteries haunting his nebulous past could be translated into forms of meaning and permanence.

No one will ever know exactly with what meaning primitive man endowed his artistic creations, but to us they are filled with magic and spirit. They may have been symbols from which spells went forth to influence hunting, fertility, and success in his various ventures. They may well indicate the first vague glimmerings of the mighty concept of immortality and the dawning of the belief that after death he and his kind would dwell in the vast vault of the unknown. Whatever their interpretation, they mark the period during which Stone Age man emerged from the dark abyss of his past into the world of mind and soul.

The waves were higher now, still coming out of the west. Elizabeth and I were forced to dodge behind islands and points in order to make any headway at all. Once we sought shelter back of a sharp ledge and there found another face of rock, but again no pictographs, only a mass of green and black lichen covering the surface, the *tripe de roche* of the *voyageurs.* That ledge made me wonder what might eventually be the fate of all the paintings in the north. Far more of a threat than vandals, who might chip the pigment off the rocks, is the slow and steady encroachment of lichens. Some of the paintings I knew are already becoming vague, and once they are covered, no one will ever find them again.

Across the channel on the way back to the Point, the whitecaps were rolling and spray dashed high against the rocks. We fought them all the way across, rounded the headland at last, and dashed into the shelter of the bay. After beaching the canoe we started a fire, and as we sat there and listened to the roaring of the gale through the tops of the trees, we wondered where the hidden paintings might be, what secret cliffs along those many miles of shoreline primitive artists might have chosen for their work.

The pictographs are evidence of man's growth in mind and of a force that over the millennia has resulted in all cultural development. It is woven into the basic fabric of the civilization he has built. The paintings at the Rock of Arrows and on Lac la Croix and Darkey are symbols of eternal striving, shrines to the spirit of man.

The Ross Light

Years ago on a canoe trip with photographer Frank Ross of the *Saturday Evening Post,* I learned something about light I did not know before. For a long time I had been aware of the magic of those last slanting rays of the setting sun but, until that memorable trip with him, I was not fully aware of their significance and possibilities. I discovered with Ross that unusual effects could be achieved during certain rare moments when the light was just right, when color and depth were accentuated to the point where ordinary scenes could become spectacular pictures. Day after day we waited patiently for the time to come, were often disappointed, but when we caught what we were looking for, it was worth all the time and effort.

Sunsets had always brought me joy and I had marveled at those almost level rays before the sun dropped below the horizon, but with him I became so completely conscious of their wonder that never again did I accept them with complacence. I discovered later that even more than the beauty of sunsets themselves, or their miraculous color effects, was a certain indefinable impact on the mind that brought a scene within the realm of unreality and gave it a patina it did not have before. In their glow came deeper meaning and dimension and, at the moment, all that was bathed in it was illumined and exalted until the vision became one of fantasy and delight.

We were paddling along through the rushes of Moose Bay off the mouth of the Robinson River when I first saw this glowing afternoon light with Ross. The shore was good for game and we watched it closely. Moose and deer often came out there, and once I had seen a bear with two cubs splash across the sand spit that separates the bay from Crooked Lake. A long beach was screened by rushes, and the spruces behind it stood tall and dark. Something moved, and there was a big buck with a splendid set of antlers wading sedately through the shallows.

Frank readied his camera and I pushed forward silently, without taking my paddle from the water. The buck was unaware. The light was bad against the darkening shore, but suddenly the sun flashed through a cloud bank and for an instant the antlers were gleaming gold and the entire scene transformed. The animal saw us and in a series of tremendous leaps headed for the bank with golden spray flying all around. The spruces were splashed with it and our minds as well. I turned the canoe and paddled back through the dusk toward camp. We had seen more than the buck, more than the light itself, and neither of us spoke.

Francis Lee Jaques once painted a lone caribou bull on a tundra shore, and there again was the light catching one tip of an antler, turning it to gold. I now studied that picture and though the entire scene was magnificent, it was the glint on that single tine which fascinated me. Without that flash of gold, it still was a great painting, but with it the scene was enhanced by something more than beauty.

Time and again since that trip I have sat in my canoe across from a stand of red pine waiting for the light as Frank and I had done. During the day, trunks have a glint of reddish brown that toward dusk may heighten and turn to deeper red or copper. But when the Ross light strikes, those boles are changed to gleaming gold, and if there are birch or aspen nearby, some of their shimmering whiteness may be washed with it until the trees shine with glowing pink. I have seen a curving shore of birch close to a stand of red pine look as though someone had dipped a soft brush in their color and stroked the fringe of an entire bay.

All who have known the mountains have waited for the alpenglow, when snow-clad peaks turn red for just a moment and glaciers and streamers of ice hang like colored ribbons from the heights. Long after the valleys are dark, those peaks continue to glow, and as the light recedes, they fade to purple and then to black with only the highest pinnacle flaming to the end.

Late one afternoon I stood on the banks of the Yukon River just as the sun was sinking below the horizon. Some ducks took off as the Ross light struck, and they rose from a river that was no longer brown and took with them from its golden surface a cascade of glittering droplets. But it was later when our plane took off that I really saw the light and what it did to the vast Yukon Valley, the great flats, the innumerable ponds and estuaries, the unending muskegs, the rims of pointed spruce. All the limitless and unending loneliness was gone and, as I looked down from high above, I was entranced with the warmth and glowing color. Every bit of water had turned to gold and, as the valley darkened, it looked as if molten metal had been spilled and dribbled over the black velvet of the land.

One of the most dramatic sights in the north is this light on a field of wild rice. Until the time of the light's coming, the rice may be yellow or even tan against the blue of the water, but when the rays strike it exactly right, the rice may turn to solid gold. I saw it happen once on Back Bay of Basswood Lake in late October. It had been a wild, blustery day with snow swirling constantly. Toward evening the sun broke through the gray clouds and, when it washed the rice beds, the fury was forgotten — the wet and frozen hands, the shivering in the teeth of the wind—and for a moment there was a sense of warmth and quiet in which I was no longer conscious of the storm. Silhouetted against the lowering sky that evening were flights of ducks, and in the shaft of light they became drifting skeins, silver as they turned, gold as they flew into the west.

Later, on the shore of Burntside Lake, I watched the new ice forming. Some parts of the bay had already closed, but before me the water was still unfrozen. It was calm, and crystal spears extended over the surface like a net. A deep, uneasy rustling came from the expanding ice of the far shore. Before long the bay would be sealed.

As I stood there the sun broke through a mass of dark clouds and etched the scene with light. The streaks of open water became iridescent, the forming crystalline spears were like splintered glass in red and silver, the channel a shifting kaleidoscope of rose and vermilion, orange and mother of pearl against the blue. I turned and looked at the border of marsh grass back of the beach, and it was pure gold, the brown windrow of pine needles along its edge awash with it. The sun dropped, and all the color was gone. There was only the sound of the whispering ice to remind me of what I had seen.

During the winter, while skiing down the Lucky Boy Trail near my home, I stopped where it leads south to an abandoned mine. At the turn stands a clump of tall spruces loaded with clusters of cones. As I rested there, I heard a soft twittering, and looking up saw that the treetops were alive with pine grosbeaks. Bracts and scales from the seed cones on which they were feeding floated down in a shower of brown. I could not see the color of the birds in the growing dusk until the sun came out and a shaft of light struck the spruce tops. During that instant the cones became masses of gold and the grosbeaks turned to Chinese red. The birds felt the warmth of that last ray and their warbling and aliveness intensified and filtered down to me, making my resting place part of their glory. The moment passed as swiftly as it had come; the spruce tops turned black, the birds lost their brilliance and then flew back into the woods. I had stopped there many times, but had never before been fortunate enough to arrive while the birds were feeding at sunset.

In February, while Burntside was still partly open, I skied along its banks. The drifts were very deep, and great sloping mounds of them lay close to the rapids. Rabbit tracks ran over them and in places partridge had walked. It was a time of bitter cold and the colors there were blue and white: blue for the water and sky, white for the snow and ice—that is, until the Ross light came. Then the open rapids became red as blood, with the snow and ice bleeding into them, the color spreading over the banks until the entire river was covered and the trees, grasses, and shrubs were black silhouettes against it.

One summer I watched a storm build up over a little lake in the Quetico-Superior. We were camped on an island covered with huge white pines and our vista lay unbroken to the east and up a long bay where the shores were rugged and stark. Tall bulrushes grew in the sand around our end of the island, and the broken stump of a tree lay grotesquely in the water close to the landing.

For an hour, great masses of snowy cumulus had boiled and churned and now their summits were tinted with color from the setting sun. Black clouds moved among them, and from their ominous depths lightning flashed and the thunder rolled until it echoed and re-echoed from the shores. It grew darker and darker, and the waters were calm.

Over the lake lay a sense of impending doom, and we made everything safe: canoes well up among the trees, tent stakes reinforced, ropes so tight they sang when we touched them. All we owned was covered; food, equipment, dry wood under tarpaulins weighted down with heavy stones. We were at the shore ready to fly for the tent the instant the wind and deluge came.

Then a strange and eerie light was over the lake and the surrounding hills, a greenish-yellow glow that was almost tarnished gold. Rushes once black were illumined now, leaned like silver rapiers as the air began to move. The stump became alive, lost its jagged contours, and was a thing of beauty against the opalescence of the water. The cliffs and pines across the channel turned to burnished copper. Then came the wind and the rain in a final, crashing rumble — and the glory was gone.

The Ross light does strange and wonderful things to all who see it and are sensitive to its meaning. No two ever see it alike, but this much is true: somewhere within it is a power that transfigures everything, even those who watch.

Campfires

Something happens to a man when he sits before a fire. Strange stirrings take place within him and a light comes into his eyes which was not there before. An open flame suddenly changes his environment to one of adventure and romance. Even an indoor fireplace has this effect, though its owner is protected by four walls and the assurance that, should the fire go out, his thermostat will keep him warm. No matter where an open fire happens to be—in a city apartment, a primitive cabin, or deep in the wilderness—it weaves its spell.

Before men ever dreamed of shelter, campfires were their homes. Here they gathered and made their first plans for communal living, for tribal hunts and raids. Here for centuries they dreamed vague dreams and became slowly aware of the first faint intimations and nebulous urges that eventually were to widen the gulf between them and the primitive darkness from which they sprang.

Although the gulf is wide, even now we can see the future in leaping flames, and we make plans in their enchantment which in the brash light of day seem foolhardy. Before the flames, modern conquests are broached and unwritten pledges made that vary little from those of the past. Around a fire men feel that the whole world is their campsite and all men partners of the trail.

Once a man has known the warmth and companionship there, once he has tasted the thrill of stories of the chase with the firelight in his eyes, he has made contact with the past, recaptured some of the lost wonder of his early years and some of the sense of mystery of his forebears. He has reforged a link in his memory that was broken when men abandoned the life of the nomad and moved from the forests, plains, and mountains to the security of villages. Having rebridged the gap, he swiftly discovers something he had lost: a sense of belonging to the earth and to his kind. When that happens, he reaches back beyond his own life experiences to a time when existence was simple.

So deeply ingrained is this feeling, and all it connotes, that even the building of a fire has ritualistic significance. Whether he admits it or not, every act of preparation is vital and satisfying to civilized man. Although the fire may not be needed for warmth or protection or even the preparation of food, it is still a primal and psychological necessity. On any wilderness expedition it always serves as a climax to the adventures of the day, is as important to a complete experience as the final curtain to a play. It gives everyone an opportunity to participate in an act hallowed by the devotion of forgotten generations.

The choice of the proper spot to build a fire is important. No place is picked lightly, for there are many factors involved. From the time man first carried a living brand from some lightning-struck stub and then discovered how to generate a flame with a whirling spindle and tinder, he was set apart. He has not forgotten, and even today everyone is anxious to help the fire builder get started. All join in the search for kindling, for resinous bits of wood and bark. How proudly each brings in his offering, what genuine satisfaction is shared when the flames take hold! As the fire burns, see how it is tended and groomed and fondled, how little chips are added as they fall away from the larger sticks, how every man polices the fringe before him and treats the blaze as the living thing it is.

Anyone who has traveled in the wilds knows how much he looks forward to the time of day when he can lay down his burden and make camp. He pictures the ideal place and all that he must find there: water, a good wood supply, protection from wind and weather. As shadows begin to lengthen, the matter of a campsite takes precedence over everything else, as it has for ages past whenever men have been on the move. The camp with its fire has always been the goal, a place worth striving toward and, once attained, worth defending against all comers.

G. M. Trevelyan once said: "We are literally children of the earth, and removed from her our spirits wither or run to various forms of insanity. Unless we can refresh ourselves at least by intermittent contact with nature, we grow awry." What he was thinking of were the ancient needs of men caught in the intricate and baffling milieu of a civilization that no longer provides the old satisfactions or sources of contentment. Thoreau implied the same when he said, "In wildness is the preservation of the world." The campfire would have typified a necessary means of contact to them both.

In years of roaming the wilds, my campfires seem like glowing beads in a long chain of experience. Some of the beads glow more than the others, and when I blow on them ever so softly they burst into flame. When that happens, I recapture the scenes themselves, pick them out of the almost forgotten limbo of the past and make them live.

One of these glowing beads was a little camp on a bare shelf of rock beside the Isabella River. The moon was full that night and the tent stood in the light of it. Because the river ran north and south at that point, the moon shone down the length of a long, silvery pool, turning the rapids at its base into a million dancing pinpoints. A whippoorwill was calling and the valley of the Isabella was full of its haunting music, a music that seemed to blend into the gurgle of the rapids, the splash of rising trout, and the sleepy calling of a white-throated sparrow disturbed by the crackling flames.

The tall spruces at the end of the pool were black against the sky, and every leaf was tinged with silver. A trout rose again and again, and widening circles moved over the pool, erasing the smooth luminescence of its surface. The campfire was part of the magic and witchery of that scene. For primitive man the night might have been tinged with superstition and perhaps with fear. I only wondered at its beauty.

One summer I made an expedition into the Maligne River country in the Quetico and was camped on a slender spit of rock overlooking the wild, island-studded reaches of Lac la Croix. A dead pine had fallen and shattered itself on the very tip of the point, and there with chunks of the resinous wood I built a fire, then sat on a little shelf of rock under the pines, where I could watch the firelight change the branches and their tracery to coppery gold. For hours I watched them and the reflection on the water, but when a loon called from the open lake and then swam like a ghost into the circle of light, the scene was touched with magic.

Another time, Dean and I were camped at the mouth of the Range River where it empties into Low Lake. The blue-bills had come and gone, and a snowstorm was raging overhead. Our tent was in the shelter of a ledge that protected us from the gale. It smelled of balsam, and our sleeping-bags were dry and warm. The little campfire out in front not only meant warmth and protection from the cold, but somehow made us part of the storm. Through it we could watch the swirling snow, hear it hiss as it struck the water, see the branches of the trees and the ground becoming whiter and whiter. Once, above its whispering and the roar of the wind, we heard the sound of wings — a last belated flock hurtling down the river.

Once, on the Fond du Lac, my Canadian *voyageurs* and I pitched our tents on a ledge of limestone high above the river with a view down the waterway for miles to the west. So steep was the approach that we were forced to drop a bucket on a line to get water. It was a campsite one dreams about: a wild rushing river below, a view into the sunset, and tremendous rock formations on either side.

The west reddened, and as we sat by our dying fire a moose came out from shore half a mile away. A bull with a great spread of antlers, it walked majestically into the shallows and began wading across, slashing the color as it advanced. On a long sandbar in the center of the river it stopped, head held high, then splashed through the sunset glow until it disappeared into the timber of the opposite bank.

One day, with an Arctic wind sweeping inland from the ice floes of the Hudson Bay straits above, it was so bitterly cold we could paddle only a few hours at a time without being forced to land and build a fire. By nightfall, wet and tired from many rapids and portages, we dragged our gear into the shelter of a dense grove of spruces and pitched our camp in an opening beneath them. Only when the fire blazed high did we discover the enchantment of the place we had found, a high-ceilinged room with a golden floor and golden rafters, the walls huge black boles of trees. Not a gust or breath of wind disturbed us as we lay basking in the warmth. The spruces moved and groaned, but we were safe from the storm, safe and snug as animals in a cave. The day's adventures — the roaring rapids, loss of equipment, the struggle against wind and sleet — were far away. We ate our food, got into the sleeping-bags, and watched the firelight on the canopy above us.

There have been countless campfires, each one different, some so blended into their backgrounds it is hard for them to emerge. But I have found when I catch even a glimmer of their almost forgotten light in the eyes of someone who shared them with me, they flame once more.

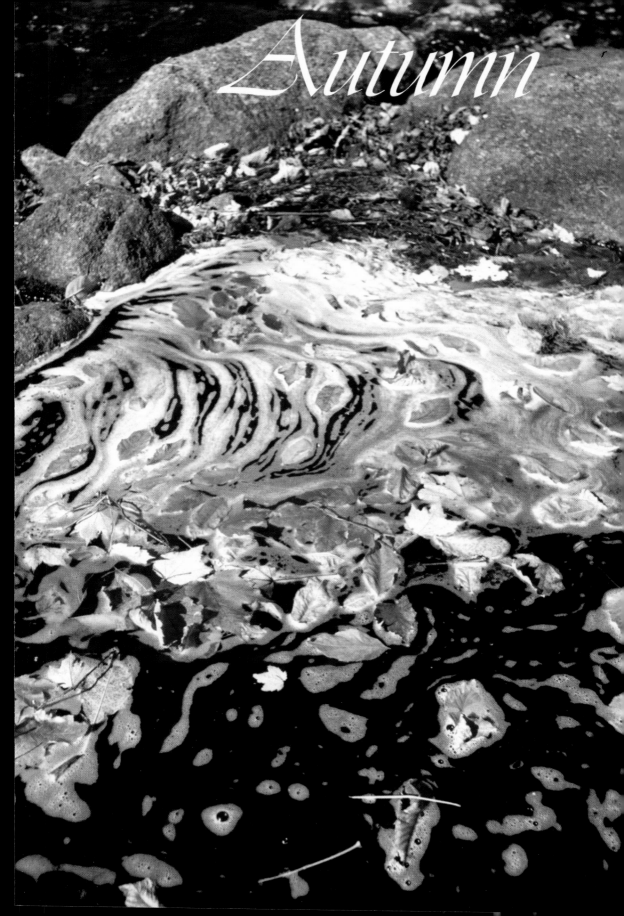

Autumn

Autumn comes without warning at a time
when the lush fruitful days of midsummer
are beginning to wane, but when it still
seems as though food, endless plenty, and
warmth must go on forever. It may announce
itself with just a touch of coolness on some
bright morning toward the end of August,
or by a few high leaves barely tinted with
color, perhaps a spot of rusty gold on the
bracken, or a tuft of grass turning sere.
All young are grown now, ready to leave
nests, spawning beds, dens, and shelters.
Then, almost imperceptibly, a burst of
activity is evident in a growing urge to store
food, in a scrambling for seeds, cones, and
dried fungi, and in the mounting piles of
birch and aspen branches around beaver
houses. New birds appear, gathering for
the migration south, and there is excitement
in the air with strange wings at dusk over
marshes and lakes, and in the sense of
little time and that all must hurry before
it is too late.
Woven through all this is the dramatic
phenomenon of color—at first hints
and flecks of it floating in the gloom of the
woods, then the bright and pastel shades of
shrubs beneath the trees, and at last the trees
themselves in such flaming magnificence it
is almost more than can be borne. The north
becomes a land of blue and gold, and skies
once more are alive with the movement
of myriad birds.
At last all the flamboyant beauty is on the
ground, on portages and in pools and along
lake shores. A somberness comes to the
land and with it a feeling of welcome quiet
and relief to all living creatures who
stay on.

Falling Leaf

It was a bright and sparkling morning in late August with just enough hint of frost in the air to make one question the permanence of summer. A blue jay screamed the hard clarion notes of coming fall, and in that sound was the promise of change.

I stood beside the big boulder on top of Listening Point. Beyond it and silhouetted against the blue of the north channel was a large-toothed aspen. A small scraggly tree, it was sparse of leaves and branches and its roots went into a crevice of the rock. Standing there alone, it was like a Japanese painting in its stark simplicity. If the blue jay was right, it would be one of the first to turn, would change while the shores were still massed with green. Unconsciously I looked toward the top and, to my surprise, the leaves seemed tinged with a faint glow. At the very top a single leaf danced and turned in a sudden breeze, then separated itself from the branch and whirled in slow fluttering circles down to where I stood. I picked it up, twirled it between my fingers, observed the prominent veining, the great even scallops along its edges, and the end of its stem, where growing cellulose had severed it from its holdfast.

The base of the leaf was yellowish green, but along the sides and tip it was tinted with peach and rose—and this only the end of August! I looked at that first color as though I had never seen such beauty before that moment. It was hard to realize that the warmth now showing through had been there all the time, hidden by green chlorophyll until fading sunshine and growing cold had stopped its production. In that fallen leaf was the story of the season's advance, an indicator of shortening days and lengthening nights.

Summer comes slowly in the north, is never fully here until the end of June, and sometimes, when June is rainy and cold, it actually seems to start in July. But to have the change begin before summer has really settled down and the leaves grown to maturity is a shock when you have waited for it and dreamed about it since the snows disappeared and rivers ran free of ice.

I remembered a flash of red I had seen two weeks before on the south shore of the lake. It had not impressed me then, for the time was mid-August and it could not possibly have been a warning. Perhaps, I reasoned, a beaver had gnawed the bark, cutting the flow of sap, or exploring roots had found a dry crevice in the rocks and the tip, being starved for food and moisture, had gone into early flame. Surely it could be nothing else, for the days were still balmy and the nights as well, and the water had barely warmed to the point where swimming was no longer an ordeal. But now I knew that the crimson flag against the solid green of the hillside had responded exactly as the leaf of the aspen had done; that, whatever the combination of circumstances, waning sunlight had hastened the change.

I tucked the lone leaf carefully into my wallet. It would remind me to be aware that summer was slipping away. The leaves in the top of the little tree shuddered suddenly in a breeze, then danced and pirouetted as only aspen leaves can. Another floated down and rested its color on a bed of bright-green moss behind the boulder.

A few days later, in the end of a swampy bay on the Basswood River I found a stand of ash turning to lemon yellow after a bare three months of growth. No wonder they mature slowly, with three months of green and nine of bareness standing in the cold, acid medium of a bog.

That same day I found a bright-red leaf of wild geranium laced flatly against a ledge of greenstone. Beside it was a cluster of pink corydalis still in bloom, and just beyond the sky blue of a single long-stemmed aster. Under the trees the bracken had changed to russet and bronze, and when I looked closely I found the entire forest floor moving slowly into color, a dwarf honeysuckle in red and a mountain maple shifting to the peach and rose that would brighten thickets until all the leaves were on the ground.

On the Robinson River I paddled to a flat ledge where the water races down toward Moose Bay of Crooked Lake. Above the break a mat of poison ivy growing in a crevice had turned, each stem and leaf shouting, "Danger—do not touch!" On an old burn just beyond, a thousand asters were in bloom and goldenrod as well, the first of the blues and golds of Indian summer before the storms came down.

By the middle of September, maples were flaming along all the roadsides from Lake Superior to the border. Mountain-ash berries hung in crimson clusters, and along the rivers the rice had turned from light green to yellow. Ducks were on the move, and on the Bear Island, the Burntside, and the Stony the whisper of wings could be heard at dusk.

Now were the days of color and of finding the places where it was best, for time does not wait in the north and a gale can change it swiftly overnight. Nothing more important now than reveling in shifting panoramas, exploring scenes remembered vaguely from the past, surcharging minds and spirits with color and warmth against the coming white and cold. There were many places to go, each one different, places that somehow had poetry of their own and, while part of the changing scene, stood out and said, "Enjoy me while you can."

One such place was in the darkness of the pines. I found it one day when the gloom was sprinkled with flecks of dusty rose and Chinese red, flecks that seemed to be floating or held in suspension. In places they were almost blown together and continuous, but even so there was a lightness and evanescence against the black-green of the pines that is never found where the sun shines directly on the trees. As I watched it, the black tracery of branches gradually disappeared and I saw what an artist might see in his painting: flecks of color and the illusion of stems without their actual portrayal.

This was the prelude, the elfin flutes and almost inaudible strings that set the tone for the bold crescendos of blue and gold and red to come. Then, with the ground as colorful as the trees themselves and the atmosphere charged with power, it would be hard to remember when the first faint hints of change drifted into the woods and the somberness was dusted with floating bits of light.

I wondered, as I lingered beneath the branches of a pine, watching the ephemeral drifts of color and the black tracery of branches, looking through them and their infinite variations, if this weren't the best of all. But I knew that here was only one muted note, that without the rest the symphony would not be complete. Even as I stood there I was conscious of deepening color far beyond the pines and along the crest of a ridge, and knew that the delicacy and evanescence was already fading, and boldness beginning to show.

I tried to hold for a little while the beauty before me, the sense of floating color and the artistry of flame against the dark, knowing it was part of the smells and sounds and rememberings of the past. Nothing could possibly be lovelier, or so I believed, forgetting that each year I had thought the same. I tried to think of the coming hush, with the leaves on the ground and all the color drained from the hills, the somber browns and greens waiting for the snow, but somehow all I could see was what was before me—a moment like a poem to be long remembered in the days to come.

One night Elizabeth and I unrolled our sleeping-bags under a full moon beneath a maple that had turned to gold, lay there and watched the light streaming through. The ground was silver and gold and the air as well. We were bathed in the glow, became part of it, and drifted off to sleep. Several times we awakened, watched the play of light above until drowsiness claimed us again.

The morning sun picked out the topmost branches glistening with frost. A single branch burst into flame, as did a cluster of brown cones in the top of a pine. We lay there and watched the lazy spiraling down of leaves. I touched the trunk of a nearby sapling and a cascade of frosted color filtered down upon our bags. Behind us crimson sumacs fringing a little glade were dusted with silver.

By mid-October the leaves were falling fast and the shorelines turning everywhere. The little bay with its cedar and aspen had changed with the rest, and islands and mainland were solid gold as far as I could see. Only in a few places was there any touch of red—on the hilltops where the scrub oaks still held their leaves and in protected bays where winds could not reach.

But along the roadsides and underneath the trees now appeared a display that until then had been hidden from view. Cherries, mountain maple, June berry, honeysuckle, and hazel all had turned to shades of red and gold. Blueberry and bearberry beneath the pines were now a carpet of crimson. Together with the fallen leaves, they made the entire forest floor a tapestry of color even richer and more varied than the trees had been. Now for the first time one could look through the woods and far into them, with vistas that seemed to stretch on endlessly into more and more color.

Even the bogs began to turn from their summer's green and brown to tones of copper, each muskeg a soft carpet, the heathers blending together to complement the brilliant shrubs that hemmed them close. The rice beds in rivers and swampy bays were yellow against the blue. Portages were deep in leaves, for all the glory that had been was on the ground.

For a month the color had been almost unimaginable. Senses had been surfeited by overwhelming beauty. Now at last somberness could come and eyes could rest, and minds as well.

Early in November I stood by the boulder where I had watched the first falling leaf come down. The leaves were all gone now, and the little large-toothed aspen stood stark and bare against the sky. The hush was already upon the land and a softness that had not been there before. Rains had come and the ground had lost its glow. It was turning brown, smelled of dampness and coming mold. Already the brilliant leaves were turning into duff and soon would be part of the black humus underneath, lending their richness to the earth and color for autumns of the future.

The leaf I had pressed six weeks before, though now dry and sere, still had its shades of peach and rose, and was almost as beautiful as when it had fluttered down before me. It reminded me of those drifting flecks of color in the deep pines one misty morning, of flaming roadsides all the way to Lake Superior, of a night when the moon was full and we lay under a maple, drenched in its golden light. In that little leaf was all the poetry of fall, the first soft prelude of the symphony just finished. The cycle was complete once more. Now the snows could come.

Wild Rice

When I look at my bag of wild rice, I feel rich. Food of the north, this is nature's wheat, the traditional staple of Indians in the lake states. True, they have many other foods, but this wild grain, gathered in the shallow, mud-bottomed lakes and rivers of the north Middle West, is more important to them than any other. Bloody tribal wars were once fought for its possession. Those whose lands included stands of it were considered wealthy and insured against starvation and want.

Wild rice is easy to prepare: it needs only to be washed, to have boiling water poured over it, and be allowed to steam to make it palatable. It should never be boiled, for that may result in a gray, gluey mass, unless it is mixed with meat or fat. As a stuffing for wild ducks, as a side dish, or cooked with game or fish it is superb. Even for breakfast, with berries, cream, and sugar, it could give modern cereals severe competition. It can even be popped like corn in a skillet, or mixed with bacon, mushrooms, or cheese. It can be served as an entire meal or in infinite combinations with other foods. A purely American dish, it is indigenous to the north.

"Give me five hundred pounds of rice," said my friend Henry Chosa, "and I can feed my family for a year. A few fish now and then, some snared rabbits, a bear and some venison, and there's nothing to worry about. Rice, bear fat, and fish are all an Indian needs to keep him strong and healthy."

When the fur trade began some three hundred years ago, it did not take the *voyageurs* long to discover the virtues of wild rice, and soon after it was used for barter. They looked forward to it after their monotonous diet of parched corn, pea soup, and salt pork, and eagerly awaited the time when their canoes entered the rice country of northern Wisconsin, Minnesota, Michigan, and southern Ontario, where it thrived.

While wild rice never attained the prominence of that western plains mixture of dried buffalo meat and tallow, known as pemmican, it nevertheless contributed greatly to exploration and trade. Father Marquette, on his expedition with Joliet in 1673, spoke of the tall grass growing in small rivers and swampy places, which "The Savages Gather and prepare for food in the month of September." He told how they shook the ears from the hollow stems into their canoes, dried them on a grating over a slow fire, and trod the grain to separate it from the chaff.

Radisson, in the journal of his expedition into this area in 1660, left this account: "Our songs being finished, we began our teeth to work. We had a kind of rice much like oats. It grows in the water three or four feet deep. They have a particular way to gather up that grain. Two take a boat and two sticks, by which they get the ear down and get the grain out of it. Their boat being full, they bring it to a fit place and dry it, and this is their food for the most part of the winter, and they do dress it thus: for each man a handful of that they put in the pot, that swells so much that it can suffice a man."

Many explorers and traders spoke of wild rice as excellent and tasty food. Alexander Henry stated, in 1775, that his "voyage could not have been prosecuted to its completion" without the supply of wild rice acquired from the Indians at

Lake of the Woods. Daniel Harmon mentioned, in 1804, that each year he and other traders bought from 1200 to 1500 bushels.

The French called the wild rice plant—known scientifically as *Zizania aquatica*—"*folle avoine*," meaning wild or foolish oats. From this came the name of a Wisconsin tribe of rice gatherers. Early records always speak of them as the "*Folles Avoines*," though their real name was Menominee, coming from "*Omanomen*," meaning rice, and "*Inini*," person— "people of the rice." The name Wisconsin may also have stemmed from association with the grain: "*Weese-coh-seh*"— meaning "a good place in which to live." The good place may well have meant where wild rice grows and game and fish are plentiful.

When I see my bag of rice, I think of many things, for it holds far more than food. In addition to high nutrient value and flavor, it has certain intangible ingredients that have to do with memories, and for those who know the country where it grows and have taken part in the harvesting, it has powerful nostalgic associations that contribute as much to the welfare of the spirit as to the body.

There are many legends and stories about how wild rice came to the Indian people, but there is one I like best. In the days of long ago, it was the custom for the chief to send young boys approaching manhood into the woods to live alone and prove their strength and courage. They existed on berries, roots, and anything they could find, and were told to stay out many days. Sometimes they wandered very far, got lost, and did not return. During these long and lonely journeys, spirits spoke to them and they had dreams and visions from which they often chose a name. If they returned, they became hunters and warriors, and in time took their places in the councils of the tribe.

One year, a young boy wandered farther from the village than all the rest. It was a bad time for berries and fruits and he was sick from eating the wrong kinds. This boy loved all that was beautiful and, though hungry, always looked about him for flowers and lovely plants. One night in a dream, he saw some tall, feathery grass growing in a river. More beautiful than any he had ever seen, it changed color in the wind like the waves on a lake. Upon awakening, he went to the river and there was the grass, tall and shining in the sunlight. Though starved and weak, he was so impressed that he waded into the river, pulled some plants from the mud, wrapped their roots in moss and bark, and started at once toward the village.

After many days he saw the tepees before him, and when at last he showed what he had found, his people were happy and planted the still wet roots in a little lake nearby where the grass grew for several years until it became a waving field in the bay. One fall, a wise old Indian who had traveled in many countries and knew all things came to visit the village. He was taken to the lake to see the beautiful, tall grass one of the young men had found. Seeing it, he was amazed, raised his arms high and cried in a loud voice, "Manomen— Manomen—a gift from the Manito."

He explained that the seeds were good to eat, showed them how to gather the rice and separate the chaff from the grain. Before he left, he advised them to plant it everywhere, guard it well, and use it forever. The Indians have never forgotten—and now all over the north country it grows in golden fields.

In the old days each family had a portion of a rice field as its own, outlined by stakes and established as a claim long before the rice was ripe. Sometimes as an aid in harvesting, and to protect the grain from the ever present threat of being blown off by the wind, the Indians tied it into small sheaves.

To tie it, basswood fiber was used, one length fastened to another until a large ball was made. The ball was placed on a birchbark tray behind the woman doing the tying, one end of the fiber going over her shoulder through a birchbark loop to her hand. As the canoe was pushed through the rice, she gathered it in with a hoop and with a deft motion tied it together. The rows were long, their straightness a matter of pride. Now the rice was claimed, and safe from the storms.

At harvesting time, a camp was set up on the shore of a lake or river where wild rice grew; often several families were banded together. Equipment was simple: canoes propelled by long, forked poles, rice-beating sticks, birchbark, woven matting of cedar, canvas, kettles or tubs for parching, trays for the winnowing, bags or bark containers for storage.

Few food supplies were taken along on these expeditions, the natives depending almost entirely on rice with fish, game, and berries, and maple sugar from the spring gathering was often the only seasoning. At night the women set their nets and in the morning drew them out. If fishing was good, drying and smoking racks were set up and the fires kept going constantly. The men hunted the fat rice-fed ducks; shot moose, bear, or deer wherever they could find them. Snares were set for rabbits and partridge, blueberries were picked and dried, a great supply of food laid by for the all-important days when harvesting took up their time.

Each day after work around the camp was done, the men and women started for the rice fields, usually not to return until midafternoon. A canoe full of rice was considered a day's harvest if there were any distance to go, but if the field were close, several loads could be picked in a day.

Warm, still days were ideal for harvesting, as winds and rain could ruin an entire crop within an hour—a catastrophe not unknown. This was the reason for tying the heads, for then the storms could come without danger of losing all. Not all the rice was picked; some was left for seed and some for the ducks, who were not only good to eat, but planted the rice, as they believed, in many places.

In small camps the parching and threshing was done in the afternoon and evening, and those who did the harvesting assisted; but in large camps, where several families worked together, this all-important activity was carried on by trusted experts who did nothing else.

Some years ago, in early September, I carried my canoe across the Basswood portage to Hula Lake, where I knew the Indians were camped. Long before I reached the tents and tepees along the shore, I could smell the rich pungence of the parching fires, for their haze hung over the woods and blended with that of fall. Just before I reached the camp I stopped and rested my canoe in the crotch of a tree. A dog barked, someone was chopping, and then I heard what I was listening for, the modulated voices of Chippewas talking. It was a pleasant sound, rising and falling, an obligato to the rustling of leaves and to the lazy smoke drifting through the trees, part of the hush which seems to lie over the rice beds before they turn to gold.

Continuing the portage, I walked through the camp, dropped my canoe at the landing, and returned. The men were sitting around resting and smoking after their day in the rice fields; women tended parching kettles, some tossed winnowing trays in an open place. Over a central fire was a tripod of white birch poles and from it hung a great iron kettle. An old woman was stirring, and the fragrance of a wild-rice stew made me hungry for the evening meal. Just beyond, another woman was chopping wood. Dogs and children ran happily about. Some canoes were still out, others returning loaded to the gunwales with green rice.

The field lay greenish gold in the light, and the aspen where the camp was pitched took up the color, deepened and spread it all over the shore. Flocks of ducks were over the nearer rice beds with a constant movement and flashing of wings; they paid little attention to the harvesters. Mostly black ducks, they were heavy and sluggish with the rice they had been gorging. When canoes came close, the ducks rose reluctantly to alight a short distance away, only to hurdle the canoes on their flight back. The harvest of succulent, water-soaked kernels on the bottom was also theirs. Already fat as butter, they had a flavor no other fowl could equal.

David Thompson, a famous explorer in the late seventeen hundreds, spoke not only of the rice but of the ducks, stating in his diary: "Mr. Sayer and his men passed the whole winter on wild rice and maple sugar, which keeps them alive, but poor in flesh. It was a weak food, those who live for months on it enjoy good health, are moderately active, but very poor in flesh."

However, when he wrote about the ever present ducks, he was more enthusiastic, for he said, they "become very fat and well tasted." Had Thompson known what the Indians knew, that wild rice must be eaten with fish, game, bear fat, or mixed with berries to be a complete food, he might have changed his opinion of its nutrient value.

The scene before me had a certain timelessness. Except for the fact that Indians now had iron kettles, canvas, and modern tools, instead of birchbark canoes, matting, and utensils made of cedar and other woods, it was little different from the age of copper and stone. These people were enjoying themselves. Rice gathering was never work, it was the occasion for a festival, with a sense of good feeling and industry that seemed to permeate the camp, the sea of tall grass out on the lake, and the very air itself.

I paddled out where some of the canoes were still harvesting. Joe and Frances were working down one of their rows, Joe poling the canoe, Frances using her rice sticks to gather in the grain. I sat quietly, watching. What a smooth and even rhythm, first the bending of the stalks to the gunwale, then a stroke with the beating stick—never a wasted motion, the action almost hypnotic in its effect. Already there were several inches of the long, green kernels on the bottom. In a short time they would be ready to return.

"Good rice," said Joe without stopping the movement of his pole. "Nice big rice, and clean."

He leaned down, held up a handful for me to see, let it run between his fingers into the canoe. I paddled close, felt it myself. The kernels were long and heavy, as fine a crop as I had ever seen.

"I save some for you," he said, and that fall it was his bag of rice that hung from my rafter.

Later I followed the canoes back to camp and watched the preparations. First the green rice was spread on canvas in partial shade, where the sun would not shine on it directly. Heating and mold could destroy it, so it was stirred and dried evenly, a process that took most of a day, depending on the weather.

After the first drying, the rice was parched over a slow fire, in a large kettle or tub placed in a slanting position so it could be stirred by someone sitting beside it. The heat was carefully regulated, but skill was required so the kernels would not burn or scorch. The quantity done at one time was seldom more than a peck, and it usually required an hour before it was finished. The woman doing this work felt her responsibility, for a moment's neglect or carelessness could destroy the work of many hours. She wielded her slender stirring paddle with a sense of importance, knowing the contents of her kettle might be the last should a storm or wind blow up before the harvest was finished.

Parching loosened the husks and imparted a smoky flavor to the rice. The paddle went round and round, through the rice and underneath, never still for a moment. A stick at a time was pushed into the fire, no large ones or any that might flame. The heat must be constant and slow.

But there was another and far more ancient process in use that day: green rice placed on a rack lined with marsh grass over a smoldering fire. Slower than the kettle method of parching, it dried the grain as one might dry vegetables, berries, or meat. This was "hard rice," greenish black when finished, requiring longer to cook. Keeping indefinitely, it was stored against emergencies and long trips.

After the rice was thoroughly parched by either process, it was put into a barrel or tub for the pounding, which loosened the sharp husks and prepared the grain for treading. A wooden pestle, somewhat pointed at one end, was moved gently up and down near the edge of the mortar, never pushed, but allowed to drop of its own weight. It was considered an art to finish the pounding with most of the rice whole. Broken and shattered grain was the mark of an amateur. While as good for eating as the other, something was lost in quality and appearance that was a matter of pride to the Chippewas.

The final step in the process was the treading to dislodge the fragments of husk. For this, a wooden receptacle holding about a bushel was partially sunk in the ground. A strong cross-pole was tied between two trees at a height of about four feet directly in front of it. The treading was done by a young man wearing a clean pair of new moccasins especially made for this purpose and tied tightly around the ankles.

The sole of the foot, so Indians believe, is particularly adapted to this work, being soft, gentle, and firm in its movements.

I watched a man do this all-important work, his treading like that of a dancer, his entire being in action. Leaning on the cross-pole and taking the weight off his feet, his body moved with undulating rhythm and sinuous grace. He felt the rice beneath his feet, massaged it, turned it over, almost caressed it in his attempt to separate the precious kernels from their hard and flinty husks. Before the days of wooden tubs, a hole was dug in the ground and lined with deer skin, but the process was exactly the same, a work of care, devotion, and artistry. Many Indians look with favor on the old ways, feel that to deviate too much from ancient customs means a loss not only in flavor but in the meaning of the food.

After the treading came the winnowing, and for this the threshed rice was carried to an open place where wind could sweep away chaff and hulls. It was either tossed and caught in a tray or poured from a height onto a canvas underneath. If the wind was dry and strong, and if parching, pounding, and treading had been well done, the chaff was all blown away, leaving the greenish, black kernels clean and ready for use.

The finished product was now poured carefully into bags, which were sewn tightly and placed under cover. Some was for sale to whites, or for trade with other Indians, but most was saved for winter food. Once birchbark or woven matting was used for containers, but now the bags are of burlap or canvas. Their contents were always precious and guarded well.

One night there was a dance: the rice or harvest dance. Everyone dressed for the occasion and there was much excitement and laughter. Kettles were steaming with new rice, game, and berries. The bags were placed under cover, where all could see and admire them, for the harvest was almost over. This was a night to be happy and to thank the Manito for his largesse and for a fine harvest season.

After dark, when everyone was fed and the fire built up, the drums began their rhythmic beating and the dancers took their places. At times only men danced in a circle around the fire, sometimes only women, often both, the usual stepping and stomping to the steady beat of the drums. That night after the dancing had gone on for several hours, I saw a young man, possibly more gifted and imaginative than the rest, begin to imitate the actions of the harvest, the motion of poling a canoe through the water, the graceful swinging of the rice sticks, the circular motion of the paddle in the parching, the dance of the treader holding on to his balancing pole, the final winnowing with a tray. Others soon followed the inspired one until there was much confusion, each attempting to interpret some part of the many aspects of harvesting and preparation. Finally, tiring, they relapsed into the ancient, broken half-step of all native dances, a ritual looked forward to by all the band.

I have not seen a harvest dance for a long time now, and it is possible younger Indians do not remember — or if they do, would think it old-fashioned and beneath their dignity to indulge — but those who have seen and taken part cannot forget the deep joy and meaning of such celebrations.

In the fall, when the rice harvest is on, I think of canoes going through golden fields of it against the blue of the water, the flash of ducks above and the whisper of their wings, the redolent haze from parching fires over some encampment. I remember the drums and the dancers under a big September moon, the soft voices of the Chippewas, the feeling of these Indian harvesters of the lake country for this gift of their Manito long ago.

Pine Knots

Pine knots are different from ordinary firewoods. They cannot be compared with birch or aspen or oak, for the time-and-effort cost of gathering them is beyond the realm of common sense and reason. The warmth they give is negligible, but the light effects when they burn have a quality and importance that none of the others can approach. The burning of an old pine knot is a spiritual occasion, and the possession of a goodly supply for winter nights before the fireplace is a joy.

It was late October when I made my last expedition for knots. I say "expedition" because each foray after the prized nuggets of resin is more like a hunting trip than ordinary wood gathering. You just do not go into the woods anywhere, but must know the terrain and something about the ecology of the forests in order to know where to find them. More important than anything else is to be in the proper frame of mind, to recognize their worth, and to embark in a spirit of adventure.

Ice was forming in the protected bays of the lake on the day I set forth. There was barely a quarter of an inch near shore, but enough to scratch the sides of the canoe. The leaves were gone and only in the hollows was there any remnant of the rusty bronze of the birches. Even the old gold of the tamaracks had disappeared and now they stood sere and gray in the bogs, waiting for the snow. The grasses were yellowed and in a little bay were covered with frost crystals. As the canoe slipped by, they moved suddenly in a breath of air, and the bay sparkled with millions of sequins. A lone flock of bluebills took wing from the open water, circled warily, and disappeared over the horizon.

I landed the canoe on a grassy slope crowned with birches. Here at one time grew tall pines—not that there were any stumps or logs in evidence, but the mounds that marked their falling showed me where they had lain. Underneath the leaves and the duff were the knots, hard and sound and heavy. They would burn like torches, keeping their flames as though unwilling to squander the energy they had held so long.

Near the landing I found several weathered to a silver gray, pointed spindles washed and polished by the waves until they were smooth and symmetrical. They had come from a pine that had dropped toward the water, and I could see its ancient top in the depths away from shore.

When I explored beneath the leaves, I found some sections of wood with the knots still in place. A blow of the ax and they were free for the taking. But mostly the knots lay by themselves with the brown disintegration of bark and wood still around them. I soon had a good pile of them down by the canoe.

Here was the same primitive satisfaction one finds in fishing and hunting or in picking berries. The closest thing to it in wood gathering is the stealing from abandoned beaver lodges of peeled and clean sticks of aspen that long ago served their purpose. Like finding knots, it is living off the country, bringing in something from the wilds which no one else could find for you, and something you would not want anyone else to do because of the joy of doing it yourself.

Knowing how knots were made gives them significance, makes them unique and different from any other plant structure. All pines have resin ducts through which the golden fluid travels from the roots to the highest twigs. Where branches leave the main trunk, these ducts are bent, and because of the bending the flow of resin is dammed, saturating and completely impregnating the wood fibers. The same thing happens in gnarled and twisted roots, in any place where the free flow of resin is slowed. Although a great log may crumble into dust, the resin-soaked knots are impervious to decay and stay on for many years.

That night I stopped at the cabin of an old woodsman who felt about knots and resinous wood as I did. We had in common a vast respect for pine and what it could do. Before I crawled into my sleeping-bag, I watched him go through a ritual he had followed for many years. In back of his barrel stove were several sticks of red pine, sticks as dry and full of pitch as he could find. I watched him select a piece, turn it over carefully in his hands, then seat himself with his back against the wall.

Very deliberately he shaved off the first long shavings, each one curling beautifully as it left the blade. The longer and thinner the shaving, the better the curl; the tighter the curl, the quicker the flame. The knife sliced through again and again, and with each slice the contentment on the face of my friend seemed to grow. He contemplated the pile with satisfaction and watched the shavings twist and curl as though they were alive in the warmth of the barrel stove.

"Nothing better," he said. "Got a fine smell, too." He handed me a stick to smell. "That will explode when the flame hits it," he said.

The pile of feathered sticks and shavings was large enough. He pushed it carefully away from the stove to a spot against the wall where it would bask in the heat most of the night and in the morning be crisp and ready to flame. He sheathed his knife, for the ritual was over, the same ritual that in thousands of cabins and farm kitchens all over the land had been routine for generations. Here was real work, as important in its way as the setting of bread or the breaking of ground. This was purposeful, primitive, and satisfying, and most surely promoted pleasant dreams.

How much better, I thought, would it be for city nerves if at the close of each day a man could put his back to the wall and in the warmth òf a barrel stove, with the wind and sleet whipping into a gale outside, whittle himself a pile of fragrant pine shavings. How much more serene his slumbers than if he simply checked his thermostat.

When I returned home the following day, I stored my knots in a special place where no one would make the mistake of taking them for ordinary wood. After hunting for them, packing them across the portages, and paddling them down several waterways, I would not let them be burned indiscriminately. They were reserved for special occasions when there was good talk, and music, and when the fire had burned to a deep bed of coals. Then, with the stage set for reverie, was the time to go down to the cache.

On one such night I picked a knot I knew well. A large one, it had come from a big lower branch of a pine that had grown by itself close to the shore of the little rock-bound lake where I had found the rest. That pine had been a sapling when the first *voyageurs* came through on their trading expeditions some three hundred years ago, was well grown at the time of the American Revolution, crashed to earth during some storm before the loggers moved in sixty years ago. There it lay while the younger pines around it were harvested, and disintegrated slowly as the birch came in. Its knots survived a great fire that swept the area as an aftermath of the logging, lying there hidden beneath the duff and away from the heat.

I tucked the knot in among the glowing coals, where it was quietly caressed by exploring tongues of flame. It began to burn, gently at first, the yellows, blues, and reds of the resins bathing its black surface with strange lights. Here was the accumulated sunlight of bygone days giving off its warmth once more, the sun that had shone over the Quetico-Superior centuries before we were born. Now it was ours to share, and with it all that the pine had known throughout its life. That pine knot was a concentration not only of energy but of the country itself. Burning it was the climax not only to its growth but to the expedition on which I found it.

Beaver Cutting

Just off Listening Point a small aspen had been felled. Though there were no beaver dams nearby, and none of their houses in the bay or toward the river, the tooth marks were fresh and plain. This must have been a lone beaver cruising along the shore with an eye for a succulent bit of food — an old bachelor perhaps, shunned by his tribe and living by himself. The top had been carried into the water, and only part of the trunk had been gnawed.

This was the sign of *Castor canadensis* that men had followed for three hundred years. When they carried the emblem of France, the fleur-de-lis, into the hinterlands, it was the beaver that led them on. Pelts were so highly prized during those days that they were legal tender and men counted their wealth by how many they owned. Blankets, guns, and supplies were rated by their worth in fur, and even today the famous Hudson's Bay blankets carry the traditional mark of three or four points, indicating the number of hides it took to buy them. While there were other furs, the beaver set the standard and it was in search of them that expeditions set out for the northwest.

Radisson and Groseilliers are thought to have visited the country north of Lake Superior as far back as 1660, searching for new trapping grounds and Indians who would trade. From that time until well after the Revolutionary War this was prized beaver country, and no one knows what fortunes in fur were packed across its portages to the waiting flotillas of canoes on Lake Superior. It was the beaver that opened up the routes of exploration.

By the last quarter of the nineteenth century, however, the trade had declined and beavers all but disappeared in the Quetico-Superior country. It may have been due to over-trapping, lack of food, or possibly disease. Not until the aftermath of logging and its inevitable fires that brought back their favorite food, the aspen and birch, did they return. By the 1920's they were well on the way to recovery, but not until 1939 was there an open season on beaver on the United States side of the border. Between that time and 1955, according to area biologist Milton H. Stenlund, 166,785 beavers were taken in Minnesota, with a total value of three million dollars. It is of interest to note that the last year of record, 1955, showed the most pelts: a total of 22,500, proof of the durability of the species.

Beavers are highly important to the ecology of the north. Their ponds provide habitat for black mallards and wood ducks, forage and refuge from flies for deer and moose. Flowages and dams act as flood controls and water storage, and foresters depend on them during fires as barriers against the flames.

Trout fishermen are divided in their opinions. Some say that streams are improved because back of every dam is a pool. Others bemoan the fact that dams eliminate fast water— all the ripples and natural swirls that harbor trout—and that eventually all trees beside a stream are either cut by beavers or killed by flooding.

The fact that an adult beaver may down as many as a

hundred trees in a year shows what damage to forest cover can take place, explains why colonies are doomed almost as soon as they are established because of the vast quantities of food they need. After a few years, all trees within reach are gone, including stands at the far ends of canals leading from the ponds. Then the colony must move to an untouched area, to return only when new growth has come back around the homes they have abandoned.

While they have enemies—wolves, coyotes, and bobcats, and in the old days the wolverine—because of the nature of their habitat they have little to fear. Nothing can touch them all winter long while their houses are frozen solid, nor during the summer if they stay close enough to water. Their greatest enemies are disease and lack of food. When fires are kept under control and the pine and spruce grow tall, the beavers face their end. Only when aspen and birch come in do they thrive for long, and so it must have been in the early days. Tremendous fires between the stands of virgin pine produced their breeding grounds, and when these were exhausted the trade declined.

I examined the fresh cutting, the little pile of white chips that lay around the base of the stump, the peeled branch that lay silvery white in the water just offshore. Across the channel to the west was a colony, I knew, one of hundreds that now dot the canoe country. It was high time I visited the beavers again, and now I had a visit to return. I paddled across the bay and, at the mouth of a creek coming down from the northwest, beached the canoe and hiked upstream until I came to the dam. It was late when I got there, and the water lay like a pool of wine among the birches. The house rose in conical splendor in the very center of the pond, the dam curving smoothly against the flow. Though it was not large, generations of beavers had worked there building this wilderness bridge across the creek. From its mud-encrusted walls came a constant trickling, the overflow from the pond above. The water was high and into the trees, and dead birches stood knee deep around the edges. They stood there white and broken and ghostlike against the wall of black spruces behind them.

I thought, as I sat there, of the tremendous dam on Longstaff Creek to the south. It is very old, and no beavers have been there for many years. A quarter of a mile in length, it is wide enough on top for a team of horses and a sleigh, and the grassy meadow above is over a mile across. That dam is of the past, dated from the days of Radisson and Groseilliers. The meadow with its black rich soil might someday make a farm, but now it lies unused with the little creek winding lazily through it on its way to the lake.

To make the beavers work on the dam below me, I broke through its crest, tore out several poplar sticks and stones, and kicked away the mud. Soon the water surged noisily through the gap, a challenge the beavers could not ignore.

I climbed the hillside then and settled down to wait. Perhaps they might cut some aspen right before me, drag the branches to the dam, and carry armfuls of mud to hold them down. Suddenly a head showed near the break, and a beaver climbed out and made a survey. Soon there were others, and then I heard the sound of a tree being felled. I could not see, for it was dusk, but there was a swish, and a small tree fell to the ground; more gnawing, and beavers were swimming toward the break with branches held firmly in their teeth. Up into the gap they went, then, and with great splashing and commotion dove below for mud. After a while there was no further sound of rushing water, and I could hear the beavers swimming and working their way up the canals toward the aspen grove and coming back again to the storage pile beside the house.

Waiting on the hillside watching the changing color in the pool, my notebook was forgotten and I was conscious only of the wild yet placid beauty of the scene below. Such scenes had taken place before Columbus ever dreamed of a new continent. Here was primitive America, and in this little valley there had been no change. While the continent had been tamed and harnessed to the will of man, here time stood still.

Suddenly it was dark on the hillside, but I sat a long time listening to the activity below me, stayed until the dankness of the beaver pond and the lushness of the flooded shores seeped into my consciousness. Then back over the darkening trail I went, back to the canoe and to the Point. By the light of the fire I opened my notebook and found only one notation, "Beaver Pond," and that was all—not one scientific observation. But I had paid my respects and lived for a while in the beaver country of my travels and thought of old Beaver Creek, which runs past my home and through the little town where I live.

Beaver Creek is marked by a fringe of alder and willow winding its way through the valley. From my home I can see the bog from whose seepage it stems. Now it is thickly grown with ash and spruce and tamarack, and along its edges are hosts of invading aspen and birch. But there are places in the deep shadows where remnants of the old cushion of sphagnum still hold on and where the earth trembles when one walks nearby. But this is only in the spring, after the melting of the snows. Only then does it resemble its former sodden virility.

The ash trees are large now, thirty feet or more in height, and they stand as ash should with their roots in the cold acidity they love. But the creek that once foamed out is changed, and only for a few days in May is there any flow at all. I followed Beaver Creek one day in the spring and found it disappears where it enters town; the old stream bed where it once rollicked merrily as it raced down the ridges to Shagawa Lake is gone. Not a trace of the water or its course remains.

When men first came to the Vermilion Range to dig for iron, the creek emerged clear and cold from the swamp, skirted a ridge of towering red pines, and lost itself in a beaver pond backed up against the hill. Here it dropped its silt, trickled through the dam, and passed the mining camp. For untold centuries humus and peat had accumulated there as it had in the old meadow of Longstaff Creek to the west. Now it enriches a hundred garden plots and lawns where the pond once stood.

Some years ago I stopped on a street where workmen were excavating for the foundation of a house. They were down three feet or more and were having trouble with their digging, for their shovels had uncovered an old beaver dam whose sticks buried in the muck were as solid as the day they were laid down.

That was one of the dams that held the waters of the pond during the days of the mining camp, the dam that marked the outlet of the creek when the pine stood dark and brooding on the ridge to the south. Then caribou and moose came from the hills to drink and feed there, and ducks nested in the sedge along its borders. That was seventy years ago. Now on the site of the old beaver pond are streets and pretty ranch-type houses and shade trees planted in neat rows. What is left of the creek runs into a drain at the lower end of the avenue, and small boys play there in the spring.

Not long ago I walked down to the creek bed just below the swamp, stepped across on a couple of whitened stones where once was a swirling rapids. It was midsummer and there were horse tracks through the mud; algae and green scum filled them, and mosquito larvae wriggled to the surface in each little puddle. The water lay dead and stagnant in the heat.

While I stood there I pictured the old Beaver Creek pouring smoothly from the cold springs and seepage of the swamp, flowing past the pine ridge, spreading out and losing itself in the pond, and at last, as though glad of release, trickling through the dam and laughing its way through the camp and down to the lake.

Sometimes in the spring, when snows are melting fast and the gutters of the new streets are running full, nights when there is the music of running water everywhere, I feel as though the old creek had come to life again and was singing its way through the clearing of the first settlement. I think of the men who knew it then and of their dreams of the fortunes they hoped to make and the city they would build there. Now they are gone, the creek is gone, and only a few remember.

But the beavers are still in the country. They do not regret the passing of Beaver Creek, for they own many others all over the area. The lone bachelor who cut the aspen off the Point may have been exploring for the site of a new colony. Perhaps he would decide to pick the bay, with its fringe of young aspen along the shore. I could spare some there, and all I would ask in return would be a chance to watch them in the summer evenings playing around the house and to hear the pistol crack of slapping tails upon the water. After all, the bay belongs to them far more than to me. I have just come, but they have been there thousands of years.

Over toward the far point, where the lone pine stood, I heard a faint splash and saw a spout of silver as a beaver slapped its tail and dove. Then I followed the wake of its swimming far toward the open, watched until it merged with the sunlit ripples and was gone.

Smoky Gold

The leaves are gone from the hillsides, and the glory of the red maple and yellow aspen and birch is strewn upon the ground. Only in the protected swamps is there any color, the smoky gold of the tamaracks. A week ago those trees were yellow, but now they are dusty and tarnished. These are days of quietly falling needles when, after each breath of wind, the air is smoky with their drift.

I walked into a muskeg where they grew, a muskeg bedded deep with sphagnum and heather and where the ground trembled beneath me. Each tree showered me with tiny needles, and the place where I stood became a golden carpet.

The tamaracks were all of a size, for fifty years ago the larch sawfly had killed all the old trees. Not a stand escaped, and only rarely is it possible now to find any living relics of the past. In the center of the bog were a few old stubs, smooth and silvery gray but as sound as the day they had died. Those trees were good for winter nights if you wanted excitement in your fireplace. Tamarack burns with a fierce crackling and a constant barrage of spitting sparks. Here are character and individuality, a release from the cold acidity of the swamps where it was grown, a final flaunting of the energy stored under bitter conditions of existence. The tamarack matures slowly, is close-grained and tough, with fibers that are packed tightly with resins. When it burns, those pent-up stores of energy all but explode.

Not long ago I traveled through Illinois, Indiana, and Iowa, and there I found many small and isolated tamarack bogs no different from those in the north. There were the same trees with their undercover of bog plants, even the same birds and insects, the identical ecological community. These tiny relic areas — all that now remain of the forests that once were at the forefront of the glacial ice — survived intact when the great recession took place, because the ground waters stayed cold and the acid peat that was their base did not change. They are islands of the past, tiny primitive areas that once were part of the ice age. They had seen the glaciers come and go and were ancient thousands of years before they were seen by man. To me they appeared as remnants of a surviving race, tightly knit and isolated communities in the midst of a homogeneous conquering power. Constantly subjected to the influence of the invaders, they had survived because the conditions that gave them racial character had not changed.

Here was ecological integrity and fortitude, with survival due not so much to adaptation to the adversities of climate and competition as to the continuance of the basic temperatures and acidities of the bogs in which they grew. Human communities faced with the same desperate problem maintain their character by keeping alive the legendry and spiritual resources that have made them what they are. The tamaracks so far have not changed, nor have the other members of the bog community of which they are a part. The muskeg is the hard ecological core that makes survival possible. As long as the core remains constant, the character of the swamps will never change. Should it vary in the slightest, the engulfing influences of the surrounding country will spell their doom.

The tamaracks seem dedicated to the past, for they are not only relic communities but serve as storehouses of ancient vegetational history. Long before they began to grow, while the bogs that now protect them were glacial pools filling in with peat, these records were accumulating. Pollen grains from all the forests of the entire area were drifting over those pools in the spring, sifting down over the water, sinking into the cold acid peat. There they rested, layer upon layer, preserved perfectly in the order of their falling. By identifying these pollen grains, it is possible to reconstruct the phantom forests of the past. Beneath the golden carpet of tamarack needles around me was the story of every climatic change, every forest fire, every plant invasion up to the time the book was closed by the completion of the mat of sphagnum over the open water of the original bog.

One autumn I was on the Island River. It was late October and the tamaracks were as golden as they would ever be. Before me was a stand of wild rice, yellow against the water, and because it was a bluebird day* there was not a wing in the sky. I stood there just looking at the horizon. Suddenly the sun went under a cloud and it began to snow, softly at first, and then as the wind rose the serrated ranks of tamaracks across the bay almost disappeared in swirling flakes. A flock of northern bluebills tore out of the sky with that canvas-ripping sound that only bluebills make when they have been riding the tail of the wind and decide to come in. In a split second, an instant in which I was too startled even to move, there were a hundred wings where before there had been nothing but space. Then they were gone, and in the same instant the sun came out.

Across the river the gold of the tamaracks was now covered with silver, the final display of the season. The snow would strip those branches bare, but I would remember that wild flurry of wings coming out of the storm, then the quiet and the sunlight and the silvered gold of the shoreline.

In the midwestern states, it is doubtful if the relic tamarack

*A warm, sunny autumn day, usually in October.

swamps can long survive the onslaught of the bulldozer and the ditching machine. They occupy, according to economists and land experts, far more space than they should, space that might well be converted into productive farmland. A little clearing of the worthless sphagnum and heather, a few cords of rather mediocre firewood, and a good straight ditch through the layer of black peat are all that is required. Then a sweetening of the acid soil and furrows will pave the way for the worthwhile production.

When they go, we will lose not only storage basins for water and final refuges for birds and wildlife, but museums of the past, examples to shifting humans of the stability of an ecological community that has stood the test of time. We will lose much of beauty if we trade them for more farmland, and we will lose our chance to study a primeval environment, its interrelationships and dependencies.

In the north there will no doubt always be tamarack swamps, for there the stands are extensive enough to survive and are a definite part of an ecological pattern that does not include agricultural land. Their smoky gold in late October will always be a benediction before the coming of the snows.

Caribou

I had climbed to the top of a low mound in the caribou country over a hundred miles northwest of Fort Churchill on Hudson Bay. On the barren lands that morning was the feel of being above timber line, so fresh and clean was the air, so sparkling the sunlight. But here there were no peaks, no background of snowy ranges, only endlessly rolling ridges with scattered clumps of gnarled spruce between them. This is where the vast unbroken tundra of the north meets the jagged tree line known as the taiga. As far as I could see was the autumn pattern of copper, bronze, and red against the speckled blue of myriads of pools, ponds, and lakes. The land looked as though a tremendous deluge of waters had so recently covered it that there was no time for it to flow away, which indeed was the truth, for underneath is the eternal permafrost that keeps all waters from draining. Because of the ice, only the top few inches of soil thaw enough during the short summer to support life. Then, under an almost continuous sun, hordes of insects come forth, while flowers, heathers, and lichens and grasses all but explode in frantic growth before the descent of snow and bitter cold seals the land again in white.

This was the birthplace of the ice sheet that once lay two miles thick over the great bay and whose lobes spread to the south until they covered over half the continent. The terrain had been shaped by glaciers, smoothed and gouged; rivers and drainages had been disarranged. To the north, and beyond this gathering place of the tremendous snows that had formed the ice, are the Arctic Sea and islands reaching almost to the Pole. Here are no trees, only the tundra — Eskimo country, all of it, the land of the musk ox, wolf, and caribou, of seals, whales, and polar bears along bleak and empty coasts.

Only a few hundred miles to the south, the character of the country changes, trees gradually increasing in number — spruce, tamarack, aspen, Arctic birch, and jackpine — until the valleys of the great rivers are lush with them and the mossy tundras give way to swamp and muskeg. There lie the Churchill, the Nelson, the Albany, and the Hayes, once routes of trade and exploration from the Bay. They spread out into beautiful island-studded lakes, with rapids in between them, and gorges where they cut through the granite roots of the Laurentians or the limestones of ancient seas. At last these mighty rivers slow and lose themselves in the broad tidal flats of Hudson Bay, a depression that may have been formed by the massive weight of the ice.

I could see the white tents of our camp on the shore of Lake Nejanilini, where the caribou cross. The wind was rising and whitecaps were beginning to show in the narrows. Then from an Eskimo lookout on the point came a high clear call almost like the howl of a wolf. *"Cariboooooooooo — Caribooooo-ooooooooo."* Instantly figures ran to the canoes, and through my glasses I could see the dark heads of swimming caribou. The freighter canoes were pushed into the water and as they raced over the waves were almost hidden by the spray. In a few moments they were close to the herd and the wildly tossing antlers. The animals scattered in fright. A canoe ran alongside a bull; a swift pass of the shepherd's crook and the animal was drawn by its neck to the gunwale, held there firmly while an ear was clipped with a tag carrying two orange ribbons. As the bull was released, it plunged desperately to escape, its flailing hooves and lurching almost upsetting the canoe. On to the others sped the taggers, until many caribou wore orange ribbons with identifying numbers.

Some of the caribou were now swimming back to the shore they had left, others toward our camp. Eventually they would get together again and the migration would continue toward Duck Lake to the east. They swam high, heads and shoulders well above the surface, so buoyant it seemed as though they were treading water rather than swimming. A moose swims with only its head and the top of its hump visible, and so it is with the white-tailed deer, but these animals are different. Buoyed by a dense blanket of hollow hairs, they seem to float, and they use their broad, splayed hooves to such advantage that few animals in the north can equal them in speed and maneuverability.

The canoes were back at the shore, lookouts hiking toward their posts. In the space of a couple of weeks, five hundred caribou had already been tagged, more than any year before. Even so, it represented only a small fraction of the great herds that once came down from the tundras into the taiga, or land of little sticks. This was early September, and soon the animals would swing back for the rutting to the barrens from which they came. Then, with the first snows and storms, they would drift down once more to the ragged fringe of spruce for protection during the long winter months.

The caribou of the north have been losing ground for years, and the Province of Manitoba had sponsored this project in an attempt to find out not only how and why the caribou migrate but, if possible, other factors which might effect their numbers.

Early figures indicated fantastic populations, some explorers estimating up to a hundred million and diaries telling of herds coming across the tundras for weeks at a time in numbers that baffled description. As with the bison of the west, it was thought nothing could ever reduce them, but now something was happening to the caribou.

Reasons advanced for their alarming decline are fallout, overkilling by Indians and Eskimos, predation by wolves, disease cycles, starvation due to enormous fires that have destroyed the vegetation of feeding grounds, or a combination of all these. Estimates of the annual kill run close to thirty thousand, far more than their dwindling numbers can stand. This, coupled with other losses, makes the situation critical. The caribou are approaching the crisis the buffalo faced less than a century ago; the tagging is an attempt to find the answers before it is too late. The story of their migration and what happens to them en route can be vital to their survival as a species.

I spent little time at camp or with the tagging crew, wandered instead over the barren lands. I wanted to get the feel of this area in contrast to the forested lake and river country to the south. For the past month and for almost five hundred miles, I had traveled by canoe down the Churchill, the Rat, and the Burntwood beyond Nelson House this side of the Bay. I was still full of the tumult of rapids, vistas of great lakes, rugged portages between them, and was so completely immersed in memories of my expedition that it was exciting to be in a land where there were no forests, nothing to stop the view of endless and open terrain. It felt good to walk again, to stretch my legs and to get the sense of unlimited horizons.

I left the first low rise where I had seen the tagging, to follow the long peninsula separating Nejanilini from the Wolverine River and Duck Lake. This is the land where Indians and Eskimos meet, where the white fox, the lemming, and the Arctic hare meet the marten, beaver, and ermine from the forest transition zones to the south. While Eskimos used it in times past, it was really the ancestral hunting ground of their traditional enemies, the Chipewyans, or caribou-eaters, still the most primitive and semi-nomadic Indians of the north.

For thousands of years this famous crossing place for the migrating bands of caribou had been known and fought over by native tribes. According to Gerry Malaher, Joe Robertson had found what he thought was a Sandia-type arrowhead at the Nejanilini site which, if authentic, could possibly date back far beyond the points of Folsom Man.

The killing was done from canoes or on the land after the caribou had swum across the narrows. Both Eskimos and Indians, experts in the art of handling a spear, always aim for the same spot behind the shoulder and close to the backbone. A quick thrust by the spearsman pierces the lung; the spear is withdrawn and the canoe speeds on to another victim. Few caribou swim more than a few strokes before collapsing.

If the killing were to be done on shore, the hunters placed mounds of stones on either side of the landing place and at intervals inland, guiding the animals gradually toward a funnel, where, bunched together, they were easy prey to arrows or even spears. Sometimes women and children were placed between the piles of stones to frighten the caribou toward the place where the hunters waited. No doubt there was unnecessary slaughter during the early days when caribou were plentiful, but it made little difference then, as the endless herds came through as before with no apparent diminution in numbers.

But now, with the caribou population seriously depleted, killing more than are actually needed for food and clothing does make a great difference, and with the advent of the motor-driven canoe it is far easier to run down all the members of a band of swimming caribou and spear them before they can reach the shore. Not many years before, during a good migration, the shores of Nejanilini were piled high with bloated and unused carcasses.

The tundra was covered with bleached antlers, snow white and beautiful. I stopped before three great racks close together, their palmate tips a strange and lovely pattern against the autumn colors. There were hundreds of them, possibly thousands, as the killing had gone on for many years. In that climate they disintegrated very slowly and, in spite of occasional small nibblings by mice, lemmings, and other creatures, the antlers remained intact.

Cloud berries were yellow and juicy in low places, blueberries still holding on. They were small and bitter compared to those at home. Bilberries and cranberries were red, their leaves russet, copper, and orange. The flowers were gone, for this was just before the snows.

The walking was difficult, not only close to the water on the soft and spongy muskeg but on higher ground where the mounds and hummocks of caribou moss and tangles of heather made up the tundra. I headed for a ridge of gravel studded with huge boulders, settled in the lee of one to watch. I could see the lake, and could watch the canoes chasing another band of caribou. On all sides was space, thousands of miles of it reaching into the north, the twisted and gnarled little spruces of the taiga marching up the slopes.

There was a movement below me, and three caribou appeared in a narrow gully leading to my resting place among the rocks. The wind was in my favor and I froze, waiting. The first was a beautiful bull with an enormous rack; the others, cows. Then I saw the orange ribbons hanging from their ears and somehow for me the sense of the old north was gone. No longer were they of the ancient tundra, of the days of arrows and spears. These animals were managed, part of a scientific research project, specimens in the laboratory of their range.

I felt much the same as when I found a band on a wild mallard I had shot, watched ducklings which had been colored by injections of dye into the eggs from which they came, or saw a grizzly in the mountains of the west with an orange spot on its rump and a transistor inside. Must this, I thought, be the fate of all wild creatures left to us; must we in our need of knowledge mark and record the movements of all free, living things to learn their secrets? Had we now reached a point in our conquest of the earth when, because of our expanding population and human depredations, there was no longer an opportunity for other forms to live undisturbed?

I knew the answers as far as caribou were concerned, knew

if they were to survive in the face of what was happening all over the north, much more must be known about them. But at the same time I was saddened to realize that the animals before me had known the hand of man, and I was filled with remorse that in our mistreatment of wildlife such measures were necessary to save it from extinction.

The caribou were now within thirty feet, feeding on lichens, moving from patch to patch, nibbling a little from each. Constant movement was the answer to overgrazing, imperative to the continuance of the lichens, herbaceous plants, and willows on which they fed. At the tiny sound of my shutter, they were off with the smooth-gaited stride for which they are famous; and I heard the clicking of their hooves as they ran over the stony slope.

I left my protecting boulder and climbed higher to where I could see the whole of Nejanilini below me. The boats were out again, dashing like silver beetles over the sparkling surface. The winds were at their height and spray flew high, a good day for the tagging crew.

A well-beaten trail led up a draw. It was worn to the gravel, and alongside were whitened antlers and skulls from killings of the past. On one side was a trickle of water. The moss was emerald, the willows shoulder high. Flowers had bloomed there during the summer and I could see their withered tops. A side trail ran to the spring that seeped out in a steady flow from the gravel of the ridge. I knelt and drank deeply; the water was ice cold and clear. How green that little gully, how different from the dry and stony ridge. Little wonder the caribou made their path there.

I followed the route above it into a patch of dwarf spruce, where the trail fanned out and the mosses and earth were pawed everywhere. In crossing a swale of golden grass and sedge, I flushed some ptarmigan still in summer's brown and white. The cock soared up with a wild cackle that all but unnerved me, followed by the hen with half a dozen well-grown chicks. They had been feeding on berries and seeds and on the still-tender shoots of green near the sod. The hen returned shortly, did her best to draw me away, fluttered and clucked and dragged a wing, circling nervously.

Beyond, I found myself on another open hillside. Here I met a porcupine waddling its way, unconcernedly, from one clump of spruce to another. As I caught up, it stopped, sat on its haunches watching me gravely.

"Hello," I said. "You're a long way from home up here in the taiga. Better not get too far out on that tundra or you'll be in trouble."

Its black, unblinking eyes surveyed me for a long time, then it moved on, its quill-covered tail wagging from side to side—exactly like the porky that had girdled one of my red pines back in the Quetico-Superior, with the same movement and defensive motion. It was like meeting someone from home. For that matter, many old friends were around me: Labrador tea, Andromeda, bearberry, cotton grass, and caribou moss; and again came the sense I have known many times in the far north, of merely being on an extension of country I knew. As if to convince me this was true, a flock of snow buntings, twittering merrily, flew over and lit in a patch of sedge nearby. Soon I would see their familiar tan and white again wheeling in formation over the weeds in some drifted field far to the south.

On the very summit of the hill I stopped to rest. This, I thought, is how the great plains must have looked to those seeing them for the first time during the migration to the Pacific, the same limitless expanse and sea of space. There was the heavy, matted sod of centuries, cottonwoods in the bottom of slow, meandering streams, millions of buffalo, antelope, and elk. Here was muskeg, tundra, and caribou, and under it all the permafrost, which determined what might live.

I crossed a creek below the ridge and climbed a sandy esker winding across the country, a low embankment of stratified sand and gravel that seemed like a roadway, so smooth was its surface, so well shaped its curves. It looked new, as though the glacier had left only a short time before. To the south, where it is estimated the ice retreated some ten thousand years ago, all such formations are eroded and grown with trees, but on the barrens these dry river beds that once ran under the glaciers are as distinct as when first exposed. Here there is little rain and, because of the perma-frost, slight runoff and erosion. As a result the eskers and glacial moraines lie almost unchanged.

I found an Indian grave, the carved fence around it down, a weather-worn paddle across it. From this high and lonely place the spirit of the departed could survey the old hunting grounds, watch caribou as long lines wound over the hills, listen to their footsteps as they crossed the stony ridges. In those days—for the grave was very old—the lines of caribou reached from horizon to horizon, the wolves following them while hunters lay in wait; and still the caribou came, and there was always plenty of food.

Several caribou were now in evidence, two in one group, five in another. They grazed around me, but when they caught my scent began to run. Two bulls with enormous antlers held far back on their shoulders moved into a thicket of spruce. They seemed very dark as they came nearer, their ruffs and flanks startlingly white. I circled, came up against the wind, finally was close, and had I been an Indian with a bow or spear I might have killed one with ease.

Before me now was the outlet of Nejanilini, a river called the Wolverine, the route to the Seal and to the Bay above Fort Churchill. Here are foaming cascades and rapids whose waters are alive with grayling and huge trout. I followed the river for a while, looking into its pools and backwaters, hoping to surprise a bear, a fox, or even a wolverine, but saw nothing except an osprey soaring high above the channel. The wind was now blowing a gale, the clouds dark and ominous, and it began to rain, a cold sleeting drizzle that drove me into the protection of a dense tangle of spruce against the bank. I found dry branches, kindled a fire, and waited out the storm.

After I was warm and dry I started back over the hills toward camp. The muskeg in the low places was soggy now, the brush dripping, so I followed the ridges wherever I could. The blue of Nejanilini was gone. I stopped on one of the highest points and looked to the north.

In the space of a few hours, fall had disappeared and the once bright horizons were lost in swirling mist and sleet. I knew now why the caribou came into the taiga ahead of the storms. Here in these scrubby, moss-hung windbreaks, they would band together for protection, and were I a native, this too would be my wintering place, close to the rapids and its fish, close to the caribou, and out of the wind. Some day I should return, and stay the winter through, for only then could I learn the meanings of this vast and lonely land.

Hunter's Moon

When the hunter's moon of October emerges from the dusk, when it is huge and orange over the horizon, I am full of a strange excitement, filled with unrest and the urge to range valleys and climb mountains. I need vistas from high places, to see the silver of roaring rapids and sparkling lakes, to be part of the moon-drenched landscape and its continental sweep.

All life is changed then. Dogs howl madly when it comes into view and wolves make the hills resound with their wild music. Fish feed and throw themselves out of the water in sheer exuberance. Birds take to the air and sing in the glory of its light. Larger forms of game embark on galloping expeditions over their range. Under a full moon, life is all adventure.

On a high, glaciated ridge where Elizabeth and I could see the dark ranges to the east, we settled down to wait. Below was a tall stand of aspen which, in the gathering dusk, was old gold and peach, a soft diffusion of color melting into the dark. A few hardy maples still held a scattering of brilliant leaves, but a scrub oak growing out of the ledge flaunted its mahogany in triumph over the gales. To the south the lake was tinted with the sunset and beyond were the twinkling lights of Ely. Gradually the water turned to wine, then mauve, and the molten gold below faded into the darkness of the valley.

In a dark notch of the hills had come a change, barely perceptible, and as we watched, the brightness increased and the notch was plainly outlined in light. There seemed to be a boiling and stirring of vapors, such as below a falls or rapids at dawn, and within us was also a stirring, an excitement and expectancy that comes only when the moon begins to emerge, slow-moving, majestic, and filled with meaning for all forms of life including man. At such times under its magic spell I must do as all the rest, steep myself in the light until I can lie down and sleep in the full blaze of it, being true to one of the most powerful influences within me: the reaction of protoplasm to lunar force.

We must go back to the very beginnings of time to understand why this is so — back to the prehistoric, when the first protoplasmic droplets of life were responding to the powers of lunar attraction and the tidal cycles of the new world. The moon that moved oceans and changed environments sheltering life in the making had a powerful and permanent effect on all protoplasm.

During the eons that followed, this influence wove itself deeply into the entire complex of animal reaction. It is not surprising that man in his era of dawning intelligence made use of lunar periods in marking time, that the moon became not only the regulator but the mentor of his activities. Man began to feel that its various phases were good or bad, as past experience indicated. More and more it became part of the dreams and mystery that shrouded his early gropings toward the meaning of life and religion. The moon worked its magic, and for untold centuries men have greeted its rising with awe and reverence.

Is it any wonder that we still marvel at the coming of each full moon, that it makes us restless, uncertain, and adventuresome? Is it any wonder, even though we no longer depend

on it for good or evil omens, no longer govern our lives by
its appearance, that it continues to arouse strange and indefinable feelings within us? As moderns we may have forgotten its ancient meaning, but inherently our responses to
moonlight are no different from those of our ancestors — or,
for that matter, from the responses of all other living things
on the planet. It is still an occurrence of cosmic significance.

If humans in all their sophistication permit moonlight to
affect them, how much more does it affect animals? In my
own moonlit wanderings I have had abundant occasion to
see what it does and how animals in the wild respond to its
charm. I have listened to loons go into ecstasies on wilderness lakes, have heard them call the whole night through and
dash across the water as though possessed. I have heard
sleepy birds begin to sing at midnight; wolves, foxes, frogs,
and owls respond to the same inherent urge.

But the most delightful expression I know is the dance of
the snowshoe hare in midwinter. If, when the moon is
bright, you station yourself near a good rabbit swamp and
stay quiet, you may see it, but you will need patience and endurance, for the night must be cold and still. Soon they begin
to emerge, ghostly shadows with no spot of color except the
black of their eyes. Down the converging trails they come,
running and chasing one another up and down the runways,
cavorting crazily in the light.

If you are weary and have seen enough, make a swoosh
like the sound of wings and instantly each rabbit will freeze
in its tracks, waiting for death to strike. But they are not still
for long. As soon as the danger is past, they begin their game
again. Very seldom do they leave the safety of their runways
and the protecting woods, but once I found the lone track of a
snowshoe rabbit several hundred yards from cover and knew
the moon had gotten the best of him and that under its spell
he had left the woods and struck out boldly across the open
field. To make sure that nothing had happened, I followed
his track, expecting at any moment to see that foolish trail
end with a couple of broad wingtips marking it on either
side, or in a bloody snarl of fur where a dog or a prowling

fox had come upon him. But the tracks went on and on, grandly circling the drifts and stone piles of the meadow. At last they headed back to the woods, but the final jumps were wide and desperate and I knew the moon magic had worn thin. That rabbit, I concluded, must have been very young and foolish or very old and sure.

Once, when camped on a rocky point along the Canadian border with the moon at full and my tent pitched in the light of it, I was lying in my sleeping-bag, tent flaps open, studying the effect of pine needles etched against the sky. Suddenly I was aware of a slight rustle, as though some small animal was trying to climb the silken roof of the tent. Then I saw that it was a mouse scrambling desperately up the edge of the side wall. For a moment it hesitated, then slipped backward, and I thought it surely must fall. Another wild scramble and it was on the ridge rope itself, teetering uncertainly back and forth. Then, to my amazement, the mouse launched itself out into space and slid down the smooth and shining surface of the tent to the ground below.

The action was repeated many times until the little animal became expert and reckless and lost no time between the climb back and the sheer abandon of its slide. Faster and faster it ran, intoxicated now by its new and thrilling experience; up along the edge, straight toward the center of the ridge rope, a swift leap, belly down, legs spread wide to get the full effect of the exhilarating toboggan it had found, a slide of balloon silk straight to the needle-strewn ground below.

I watched the game for a long time. Eventually I stopped trying to count the slides and wondered at last how the mouse could possibly keep up its pace. As I lay there, I became convinced that it was enjoying itself hugely, that I was witnessing an activity which had no purpose but pleasure. I had seen many animals play in the moonlight—had watched a family of otters enjoying a slide into a deep pool, beaver playing a game of tag in a pond, squirrels chasing one another wildly through the silver-splashed tops of the pines. Under the magic spell of the moon, the mouse had acted no differently from the rest.

I thought that, if nothing else, moonlight made animals and men forget for a little while the seriousness of living; that there were moments when life could be good and play the natural outlet for energy. I knew if a man could abandon himself as my deer mouse had done and slide down the face of the earth in the moonlight once a month — or once a year — it would be good for his soul.

A slender scimitar of orange now sliced through the mist, first only its thin upper edge, then the whole of its rounded rim. The full moon was trembling and pulsating as it pushed and struggled upward and away from the haze which enveloped it; it was half, then three-quarters. The mists were subsiding, slipping away from their tenuous hold on the lower rim. At last the moon was free, an oval, glowing ball of orange, the hunting moon of October.

A great horned owl hooted down in the valley, *hoo-hoo-oooooo-hoo-hoooooooooo*. It would wait until the hollows were silvered with light, then glide through the trees on cushioned wings. Birds would stop their cheeping, rabbits and mice freeze in their tracks. All forms of life would wait until the danger was gone. This was a night of hunting not only for the owl, but for all predators in the north — including man, the fiercest of them all.

The moon was losing color swiftly and climbing high. Paling into yellow now, it would soon be silvery white. The tops of the aspen far below were washed with gold and silver. By midnight the entire valley would be almost as light as day.

The moon was almost white now and all around us colored leaves and surfaces were beginning to shine and glisten. Moonlight on a frosted leaf belongs to the world of the intangibles. And with that I was content, for though man might survey the shining satellite, he could never probe its spiritual impact. Hunting moons would come and go, and men watching would always be moved by their beauty and mystery to ponder deeper meanings. New knowledge could, however, lead to a greater perspective based on truth and understanding and an eventual flowering of mind and spirit in relationship to the universe as a whole.

We built our fire, a little one of small sticks and bits of

bark; put on the coffee pot. The tiny blaze illumined the gray caribou moss on the rocks, picked out a patch of scarlet sumac we had not seen before and some bearberry running like a red scar along a crevice in the ledge.

I remembered the time of another hunting moon far to the north, so far that it came a month earlier. We were camped on a rocky promontory on Black Lake between Wollaston and Lake Athabasca in Canada's northwest. It had been a day of long portages, muskeg, and fighting the wind, and we were weary as only men can be after traveling from dawn to dusk. There had been no sun all day, only dark and lowering clouds. We pitched our tents on a flat spit of glaciated rock close to the mouth of a river and at the beginning of a long portage around a series of rapids. In the morning we would carry the canoes three miles across a sandy plain grown with jackpine, followed by another portage of over a mile and a half to a boggy lake on the way to Stony Rapids Post of the Hudson's Bay Company at the east end of Lake Athabasca.

I remembered getting the fire under way and the pots on to boil while the others busied themselves making their beds and putting gear and food under cover for a possible blow and rain during the night. Several Indian canoes passed along the far shore. There were five all told, a hunting party going after moose or caribou. The canoes crept along the darkening shore perhaps a mile away, and though the Indians could see our fire they paid not the slightest heed. They, too, were late and heading for some campsite down the lake, doing what men had always done in the north with the coming of the hunting moon.

There, I thought, could be men of the ice age, or men of Europe, or Siberia, thousands of years ago. They were the men who stayed along the edge of the ice, followed it first south, then north with its retreat. Ten thousand years is short in the history of a race. Here in the far north, with the hunting moon, life went on as of old.

The canoes disappeared behind an island, and the far shore blazed with sudden light as the setting sun found a rift in the clouds. Beyond the island, the canoes reappeared and were black against the glow, the figures of the paddlers plain. Though there was still much to do, everyone left his work to join me. We were oblivious of time, watching a tableau of the past. The shore became a streak of livid gold against the black of the horizon and before it crept the line of canoes heading for their rendezvous.

A pair of loons flew overhead, their calls dying in the distance. They, too, saw the line of canoes silhouetted against the golden shore, but only we could wonder at its haunting beauty. The Indians paddled on in the last wash of light and warmth, threaded their way along a fringe of burning grasses, moving without effort. Theirs, too, was the ancient response to a brief moment of light and glory.

The sun sank below the break in the clouds, and the bar of orange light was slowly brushed with black. One by one the canoes slipped into the dusk and were gone. For a time we stood there held by the spell, for we too had slipped into the dusk with the Stone Age hunters of the north.

During the night I wakened and came out of the tent. The east was brightening, and I watched the moon climb into the sky and flood the water with its brilliance. Its path lay across the lake, and I knew to the west it was shining down the whole length of Athabasca, as it was to the north on Great Slave, and over the barren expanses of Great Bear south of the Arctic coast.

Two years later we were back in the north at the time of another hunter's moon. It had been a period of storm and cold without sunsets, moonrises, or northern lights to cheer our journey. We were above Great Bear in the Dismal Lakes country and I had stolen away from the rest and walked alone on a barren hillside. Before me and all around was the bleak and windswept country of the Arctic slope. To the east a few miles was the partly frozen Coppermine River and Bloody Falls, where the Eskimos were surprised by a party of Indians and massacred to the last, and the route of Samuel Hearne looking for a gateway to the Arctic Sea. The lake before me had been named for Father Rouvière. He had stood perhaps on this same rise, looking at the hills to the north and at the slender sand spit that almost cut the lake in two.

Sir John Franklin had come this way, and Charles Camsell. This was land they had known and explored.

Eskimo country, here roamed the caribou, the musk ox, and the barren-ground grizzly. Soon the tundra would be white with snow, but now it was a mosaic of color with cranberries and bilberries like jewels among the mosses and lichens. The vines had turned to brilliant red, dwarf willow and birch to orange. The flowers were gone, but here and there a few held bravely to their faded petals. A tiny willow no more than three inches high still had a withered and wind-beaten tuft of fuzz covering its single catkin. It had flowered late, and during the short Arctic summer barely had time to bloom before the coming of the cold. There was snow in the air and the wind from the Arctic ice was bitter and raw.

A small animal scurried past, a lemming or a ground squirrel. A flock of snow buntings drifted by, made a wide swing, dropped like leaves of brown and white beside me. Soon they would be back home in the Quetico-Superior two thousand miles away and I would watch them skim over the snow, dash into some patch of weeds to feed on the harvest their bodies and wings had shaken from the stalks. I would remember then and think of the barrens far away.

As I looked toward the low range of hills marking the divide between Rouvière and the Dismal Lakes, I thought how well those lakes had been named by explorers working up the shallow rapids from Coppermine to Great Bear, how fiercely desolate they could be until the sun shone or the moon came out. I wanted to see those barren hills shining again in the light, the waters below them a path of silver, but this joy was denied me. Knowing the tundra at the coming of the cold, I realized that as far as it extended from Hudson Bay to the Arctic islands this time was past. When the moon came again it would be a winter moon shining on a land that had changed little since the days of the great ice.

The coals of our tiny fire were fading and flecks of white ash covered them. While it had blazed we watched a hunter's moon and caught a vision of its light over the whole north from the Quetico-Superior to the frozen Arctic.

Scrub Oak

Elizabeth and I brought the maples into the yard so that we could enjoy for a few short autumn days the brilliant reds and yellows of their coloring, reminding us of the flaming pageantry of the entire north whenever we looked their way, the poetry of shorelines and protected bays, the magic of a lone and vivid splash of red against a whole hillside of somber green. We wanted them to remind us of the portages of October and old logging roads carpeted with their fallen leaves. The maples are finished swiftly, and when their sudden ecstasy is over they stand bare and gray with nothing to soften the rigidity of their branches. But in the spring they are again the first, with bursting crimson buds as brilliant as those of any flowers in the north.

We brought the aspen in for special reasons all their own. They are warm and friendly trees, and in the whispering of their leaves all summer long is a sense of gentleness. Although they are not long-lived, they will grow almost anywhere in open sunlight. The wood is soft, having neither the hardness of the maple nor the strength of pine, but back in the bush country the beaver depend upon it for food and canoemen for the finest firewood in the lake regions. Beaverwood, dry for many years on top of some old abandoned house — what better smokeless flame can a man want for his reflector oven, what greater cheer than its bright and eager burning? It is in the fall when the aspen's leaves are masses of old gold and the hillsides and islands are mirrored in a sea of blue that the days become enchanted and a hush lies like a benediction over the entire country. Our clump of aspen would bring us all that.

We brought in the white birch because we wanted memories of immaculate stands of them straight and white against the brown of hillsides. We wanted to remember how they looked in midwinter when under the light of the moon they changed to misty silver, ephemeral against the snow. We wanted to watch them in the spring, when the massed brown of winter slowly changed to the warmth of purple and mauve as the sap began to flow. They would tell us, too, of the part they played in the drama of discovery and exploration, for without great stands of birch there would have been no bark canoes, no *voyageurs* and their brigades from Montreal and Quebec, no Grand Portage, no fur trade in the far northwest. Most of all, they would speak of places we loved — of Hula Lake, perhaps, on a sunny day in October when the rice beds of the Chippewas lay like a golden carpet over the blue of the water and the birches at the end of the portage stood white and gold against the sky.

And now we wanted one more tree, a tree different from all the rest, with a personality and character of its own. It would not be a tree that gave much color to the country in the fall, or one that was startlingly beautiful in the spring. Those qualities we already had in the maple, the aspen, and the birch. What we wanted now was a little scrub oak, one that combined certain qualities that none of the others had, an oak that held its leaves, that had grown where survival was tough and at the end of the year flaunted a bit of color when all the rest of the trees were drab. It could not be just an ordinary scrub oak, but the best of its kind, for what we wanted to bring into the yard this time was far more than just another tree.

Leaving home one morning in late October, we paddled through several lakes toward a high, rocky ridge where we knew the scrub oaks grew. A storm had stripped the color from shorelines and islands, and where a short time before the maples had flamed and the hills had been golden, there was now no remnant of the glory they had known. As we drifted toward the ridge we searched the shores for a last cluster of leaves that might have withstood the storm, some little oak tougher and more resistant than all the rest.

In the shallows were the remains of color, yellows and golds and reds, moving slowly, shifting position with the movement of the water, covering the bottom with an ever-changing kaleidoscope of pattern and light. And then far up on the ridge we found what we were looking for, a lone spot of dark red, a final gesture of defiance to the storm, the only bit of brightness in that whole blended fusion of grays and browns and greens. We beached the canoe and began to climb, discovering that the way was hard—sheer cliffs, tangled gullies grown with hazel, windfalls one on top of another all the long climb up. At last we emerged on a smooth, barren ridge, and there was a small clump of scrub oak, its leaves still intact, their dark and shining mahogany a triumphant banner over the deserted battlefield. Whipped by many storms, the little clump had been beaten into a shape that seemed to embrace the glaciated knob of granite on which it grew. This was what we wanted. Here were character and strength.

Below us was a rice-filled river flowing into the lake. Where the stream met open water, the rice fanned out like a golden apron, solidly colored at the gathered waist, flecked with blue toward its fringes.

Then out of the north came a soft, melodious gabbling that swelled and died and at times was completely lost. High above we saw them, a long skein of dots undulatin 'ike a floating ribbon pulled toward the south by a cord tied . ɔ the point of its V. Soon the geese were overhead, and as they saw us on the ridge, pandemonium broke loose, the din of their calling so deafening it bounced off the barren rock.

Then they were fading, their calling growing fainter and fainter until at last they were gone. There was the lake with the rice-filled river running into it, and beside us the little oak now forever part of the wild pageant we had seen.

The clump was growing from a crevice in the rock, its roots penetrating deep into the ledge itself, exploring hidden pockets of humus and moisture, twining themselves so tightly into the bed rock that no winds could ever pull them free. No other trees were there—no maple, aspen, or birch. They needed far more than the ridge could offer. That hard little hilltop belonged to the oak alone.

We sat beside the clump and studied it. It had a toughness and a certain wirelike hardness that all the others lacked. The species actually seemed to thrive upon adversity and to seek out places where survival was a struggle: the rocky, sandy, windswept environments where the elements combined to dwarf and limit all other growth by making life almost impossible. We had watched the oaks in the spring and all through the seasons. Only after the more frivolous species had gone into the first wild abandon of bursting buds and flowers did they bestir themselves. Even then they leafed out cautiously, as though not quite trusting the first warm zephyrs from the south. Then, during the short summer months, while the rest of the trees and shrubs were luxuriating in an abundance of fertility, they fought for existence so that the leaves they finally brought forth might get their rightful inheritance before the cold winds of autumn fell upon them.

The aspen, the birch, and the maples colored almost overnight, but the oaks, conservative to the end, slowly turned to deep and shining red and finally to a waxy, gleaming mahogany. But when the storms came out of the north and the brilliant ones stood stripped and bare, the oaks were fully clothed and far more beautiful than the rest had ever been because they stood alone.

The clump itself was far too large to move and the roots too deeply entwined in the crevices of the rock. Walking around it, I looked for a stray shoot that might have grown from a root or sprouted from a buried acorn. I found exactly what I wanted, a tiny dwarf of a tree growing well away from the main clump. I examined it closely, for I did not want to make a mistake and touch it unless I was sure it had a chance of survival. Not more than eighteen inches high and a quarter of an inch in diameter at the base of the stem, it was well shaped and had three full-sized mahogany leaves at its tip. I felt around its base and found that the roots were completely grown into a single fissure filled with the long accumulation of humus from mosses and lichens. While a few of the finer roots had gone deeper, the bulk of them were tightly entwined around the soil of the crevice.

With my knife I sliced carefully around its edges, loosened the tight net of roots from its holdfasts to the rock surfaces, then lifted out the complete mesh without losing or destroying any part of it. Wrapping the tiny bundle of roots and humus in a bandanna, we started down the ridge toward the canoe realizing we had a prize, that in our hands was the spirit of all the scrub oaks of the north.

We planted the oak in a corner of the stone wall close to the boulders so it would feel at home and have some protection while it was resetting its roots in the glacial gravel of the ridge on which we live. When the soil was packed around it, we watered it and covered the bruised earth with leaves and grass so it would look as though nothing had been disturbed.

When finished, we surveyed our work. A single leaf remained as a reminder of the hilltop where we had found the tree, one tiny fleck of color by the wall. No winter winds would ever break this tree's branches. They might bend and twist with the sleet and snow, but they would never break. It would stand there as a symbol of the indomitable—proof that a tree can learn to live with adversity. This oak would be an antidote for softness in our environment, a contrast to the summer lushness of other trees, of grass and flowers. While they had their brief sway of glory, it would be building up its strength, and only when they were forgotten would it come into its own.

It would grow slowly, consolidate its new position, and be there in its corner long after we were gone and perhaps long after the other trees had died. In time it would be as large perhaps as the mother clump from which it had sprung. It would always stand there before the coming of the snows, holding on to its final bit of color. And those who knew its story would remember the barren ridge from which it had come and the reason for its planting.

Winter

Winter is the time of year toward which
all that has gone before seems but a
preparation. Spring means awakening;
summer, growth and the building up of
reserves of strength and energy; autumn
with its excitements and color, a violent
climax to softness and plenty; winter, a quiet
acceptance of what is to come.
When the leaves are down at last, when
reds and golds and blues are gone and the
earth has changed to browns and grays
and the air is rich with the smell of damp
and mold, the stage is set. It may come on
some quiet day in early November with
a hush so deep and so profound it seems
to press on everything. All living creatures
feel it. They watch the skies and wait.
Suddenly the air is white with drifting flakes
and tension drains as the ground is speckled
with white. The first crystals rustle as they
settle onto leaves and into crevices, and
then almost magically the earth is white
and winter has come.
Those who sleep the cold months through are
already in dens or caves, or under windfalls:
the bears, the chipmunks, the frogs. Those who
stay awake—squirrels and rabbits, foxes and
wolves, weasels and mice—are busy as ever,
and soon their tracks are everywhere as the
search for food goes on. Partridge are in
aspen tops feeding on buds, beaver snug in
their frozen conical houses feeding on
branches below the ice. Deer move into balsam
and cedar thickets and blue jays call a challenge
to the frozen world. When the bitter cold
comes, many will die in the frozen beauty of
silver and blue, but life goes on. This is a
time of survival, when only the strong will
see the spring.

Coming
of
the
Snow

The earth is rigid, the waterways are hard and blue. Aspen and birch are bare traceries against the sky, spruce and pine dark masses against the mauve of the hills. Hollows are deep in leaves. They are damp, and smell of wetness and the beginning of mold. There is a sense of expectancy, a waiting and a breathlessness. The rustling sounds are gone, the scurryings and small, dry movements of fall. There is a hush, a deep and quiet breathing after the hurried and colored violence of the months just gone. Birds are moving and squirrels storing the last of their winter's food. The ice on the lakes has secured the shores and islands, has adjusted itself to the form it must keep until spring. The woods are ready, and as the zero hour approaches, an even greater silence settles down over the north.

There is a moment of suspense when the quiet can be felt, when it presses down on everything. Suddenly the air is white with drifting flakes, and the tension is gone. Down they come, settling on the leaves, into crevices in bark, on the lichen-covered rocks, disintegrating immediately into more and more wetness. Then almost magically the ground is no longer brown, but speckled with white. Now there is an infinitesimal rustling as the flakes drift into the leaves and duff. Swiftly the whiteness spreads, then the earth is sealed and autumn is gone.

Now there is great activity among the birds and squirrels. Chickadees, nuthatches, and pine siskins are everywhere. Squirrels race madly to finish their belated harvest. There is new excitement in the air, a feeling of release. Life will now be lived in an established white world, where conditions of food and shelter will not change for a long time. Stability has come to the north and to my own life as well.

The coming of the snow adds zest to my activities. Now there will be time for a multitude of things which during the feverish moving about of summer and fall were denied me, and leisure after the long and constant busyness. To me that is the real meaning of the first snowfall—not a cessation of effort, but a drawing of the curtain on many activities. The snow means a return to a world of order, peace, and simplicity. Those first drifting flakes are a benediction, and the day on which they come is different from any other in the year.

One morning after this first heavy snowfall I took to the woods. The temperature was down, the snow deep and drifted where the wind had gone. No longer were the grasses showing or the long, sere stems of weeds. Logs and stumps and low-growing shrubs were now completely covered and the ground was smooth and white. Balsams and spruces were heavily laden and some of the birches were bending low. There was no track of any kind, not a sign of life in the frozen stillness around me.

As the sun came over the ridge, it changed the snow and its purple shadows to sparkling silver. The temperature was zero and the trees were crisp and starched with frost. There was no sound but the soft *swish-swish* of my snowshoes and the creaking of their thongs as I broke the trail.

On the sunny side of a ridge I stopped to rest, for the snow was deep and not well packed. There I discovered that I was not alone. A blue jay flew across an opening before me, a streak of blue flame against the glistening white. He perched in an aspen nearby, where I could admire his black highwayman's mask, his black and white wing bars, his vivid, icy blue. He gave a hard, brazen call, more of a challenge than a song, a challenge to the storm and cold. There was jauntiness and fortitude, announcing to me and to the whole frozen world that where there is wine and sparkle in the air, it is joy to be alive. I liked that jay and what he stood for. No softness there, pure hardiness and disregard of the elements.

A flock of pine siskins dashed into the spruce tops and scurried around busily, exploring the cones for seeds. Black-capped chickadees were also high in the trees, where they could catch the first warming rays of the sun. How merry they all were and full of life and song!

A little farther on a red squirrel scolded me from a pine stub. His twin tracks led from beneath a log, where he had been sleeping during the storm. He was out now to find the pine cones he had buried so carefully in the leaves and duff before the coming of the snow. He would find some of them, but not all—and thereby live up to his name as the greatest forester in the north, the largest planter of pine trees on the continent. He wasn't quite sure what to make of me, and stomping his feet, chattering and scolding, looking me over first from one side of the stub and then from the other. When I didn't move, he came down head first, a jerk at a time, poised for a moment wide-eyed and alert just above me, and then with a wild flurry of tail dove for his hole.

Down in the valley I saw the tracks of a snowshoe rabbit,

just a short track leading from one white-mounded windfall to another. A longer excursion in the heavy snow might have been dangerous, for now the great horned owl was hunting every night, watching the unbroken white for any sign of movement. Although the snowshoe hare is white, his black eyes give him away. He is wise to stay under cover until the snow packs or until some bright moonlit night lures him recklessly into the open.

I left the hills and headed for the cedar swamp down below. There I found the deer tracks I expected, heading for the protection of the lowlands. Along well-beaten trails they would make, the deer would feed on the low-hanging cedar that is their winter food. By spring there would be a distinct browse line as high as they could reach, not only in the swamps but along the shoreline of every lake and pond. So important is the cedar as winter food that it is often the determining factor in survival.

Along the edge of the swamp a partridge exploded out of a drift, burst like a bomb within a foot of my snowshoes, and flew into the top of a tall aspen, where it proceeded to bud as unconcernedly as though this was the normal way of getting out of bed. Survival in the cold is simple for the grouse. Long ago they must have learned that down and snow mean warmth. The only trouble with the plan was that foxes and coyotes and weasels knew it too, knew where to pounce at the ends of the short trails leading into the drifts.

A little muskeg lay below me, a place where the cranberries grew and their long, delicate vines interlaced the sphagnum. The hummocks were covered and the entire surface of the bog was smooth as any floor. Beneath that surface was a jungle of grassy roots and stems, tiny mountains of sphagnum, forests of heather, the whole interwoven with thousands of twisting burrows of meadow mice. They would not see the sun for months, would live in a shadowy blue-and-white translucency, safe from storms and hawks and owls. Only the weasels could follow them there, and sometimes the probing nose of a fox. Theirs was a world removed, an intricate winter community, self-sufficient and well organized.

Life had changed for every living thing in the north. Mating and nesting and the rearing of young were over. There was only one great problem for all: how to survive the deep snows and the long, bitter cold. For some the answer was sleep, with stored fat the source of energy and warmth. For others there was still the constant and never-ending search for food and shelter.

It is true that simplicity and order had come to the wilderness and a quiet that the months since spring had never known. There was joy and beauty in the winter woods, but there was also suffering and death. Only the strong would survive to bear their young in the spring. All forms of life prepared for it, accepted the new austere environment without panic.

The blue jay called again and I caught one brilliant glimpse as he flashed beneath the trees. Gay and cocksure as ever, he had no cares or worries as to his place in the wilderness picture. For him there was no calm resignation or concern with peace. Whether or not he survived today, this moment he would tell the world what he thought and challenge all comers, including the snow and the cold.

Northern Lights

The lights of the aurora moved and shifted over the horizon. Sometimes there were shafts of yellow tinged with green, then masses of evanescence that moved from east to west and back again. Great streamers of bluish white zigzagged like a tremendous trembling curtain from one end of the sky to the other. Streaks of yellow and orange and red shimmered along the flowing borders. Never for a moment were they still, fading until they were almost completely gone, only to dance forth again in renewed splendor with infinite combinations and startling patterns of design.

Fall Lake lay like a silver mirror before me, and from its frozen surface came subterranean rumblings, pressure groans, sharp reports from the newly forming ice. As far as I could see, the surface was clear and shining. That ice was something to remember here in the north, for in most years the snows come quickly and cover the first smooth glaze of freezing almost as soon as it is formed, or else the winds ruffle the surface of the crystallizing water and fill it with ridges and unevenness. But this time there had been no wind or snow to interfere, and the ice everywhere was clear—seven miles of perfect skating, something to dream about in years to come.

Hurriedly I strapped on my skates, tightened the laces, and in a moment was soaring down the path of shifting light that stretched endlessly before me. Out in the open, away from shore, there were few cracks. Stroke—stroke—stroke— long and free, and I knew the joy that skating and skiing can give, freedom of movement beyond myself. But to get the feel of soaring, there must be miles of distance and condi- tions must be right. As I sped down the lake, I was conscious of no effort, only of the dancing lights in the sky and a sense of lightness and exaltation.

Shafts of light shot up into the heavens above me and con- centrated there in a final climactic effort in which the shifting colors seemed drained from the horizons to form one gi- gantic rosette of flame and yellow and greenish purple. Suddenly I grew conscious of the reflections from the ice itself and that I was skating through a sea of changing color caught between the streamers above and below. At that moment I was part of the aurora, part of its light and of the great curtain that trembled above me.

Those moments of experience are rare. Sometimes I have known them while swimming in the moonlight, again while paddling a canoe when there was no wind and the islands seemed inverted and floating on the surface. I caught the moment once when the surf was rolling on an ocean coast and I was carried on the crest of a wave that had begun a thousand miles away. Here it was once more—freedom of movement and detachment from the earth.

Down the lake I went straight into the glistening path, speeding through a maze of changing color—stroke—stroke —stroke—the ringing of steel on ice, the sharp, reverberating rumbles of expansion below. Clear ice for the first time in years, and the aurora blazing away above it.

At the end of the lake I turned and saw the glittering lights of Winton far behind me. I lay down on the ice to rest. The sky was still bright and I watched the shifting lights come and go. I knew what the astronomers and the physicists said, that they were caused by sunspots and areas of gaseous disturbance on the face of the sun that bombarded the earth's stratosphere with hydrogen protons and electrons which in turn exploded atoms of oxygen, nitrogen, helium, and the other elements surrounding us. Here were produced in infinite combinations all the colors of the spectrum. It was all very plausible and scientific, but tonight that explanation left me cold. I was in no mood for practicality, for I had just come skating down the skyways themselves and had seen the aurora from the inside. What did the scientists know about what I had done? How could they explain what had happened to me and the strange sensations I had known?

Much better the poem of Robert Service telling of the great beds of radium emanating shafts of light into the northern darkness of the Yukon and how men went mad trying to find them:

Some say that the Northern Lights are the glare
  of Arctic ice and snow;
And some that it's electricity, and
  nobody seems to know.
But I tell you now—and if I lie, may my lips be
  stricken dumb—
It's a mine, a mine of the precious stuff
  that men call radium.

How infinitely more satisfying to understand and feel the great painting by Franz Johnson of a lone figure crossing a muskeg at night with the northern lights blazing above it. I stood before his painting in the Toronto Art Gallery one day and caught all the stark loneliness, all the beauty and the cold of that scene, and for a moment forgot the busy city outside.

I like to think of the lights as the ghost dance of the Chippewas. An Indian once told me that when a warrior died, he gathered with his fellows along the northern horizon and danced the war dances they had known on earth. The shifting streamers and the edgings of color came from the giant headdresses they wore. I was very young when I first saw them that way, and there were times during those enchanted years when I thought I could distinguish the movements of individual bodies as they rushed from one part of the sky to another. I knew nothing then of protons or atoms, and saw the northern lights as they should be seen. I knew, too, the wonderment that only a child can know and a beauty that is enhanced by mystery.

Now as I lay there on the ice and remembered these things, I wondered if legendry could survive scientific truth, or if the dance of the protons would replace the ghost dance of the Chippewas. I wondered as I began to skate toward home, if anything—even knowing the physical truth—could ever change the beauty of what I had seen, the sense of unreality. Indian warriors, exploding atoms, beds of radium—what difference did it make? What counted was the sense of the north the aurora gave me, the loneliness and stark beauty of frozen muskegs, lakes, and forests.

On the way back there was a half-moon over the cluster of lights in the west. I skirted the power dam at the mouth of the Kawishiwi River, avoiding the blaze of its light on the black water below the spillway. Then suddenly the aurora was gone and the moon as well.

Stroke—stroke—stroke—the shores were black now, pinnacled spruce and shadowed birch against the sky. At the landing I looked back. The ice was still grumbling and groaning, still shaping up to the mold of its winter bed.

Timber
Wolves

I could hear them plainly now on both sides of the river, could hear the brush crack as they hurdled windfalls in their path. Once I thought I saw one, a drifting gray shadow against the snow, but it was only a branch swaying in the light of the moon. When I heard the full-throated bawling howl, I should have had chills racing up and down my spine. Instead, I was thrilled to know that the big grays might have picked up my trail and were following me down the frozen highway of the river.

It was a beautiful night for travel: cold and still, the only sound the steady swish and creak of my snowshoes on the crust. There was real satisfaction in knowing the wolves were in the country and that it was wild and still big enough for them to roam and hunt. That night the wilderness of the

Quetico-Superior was what the *voyageurs* had known two hundred years before.

Some months before, I had had the same kind of experience on a pack trip in the Sun River country of Montana. In the bottom of a canyon I saw the fresh track of a big grizzly in the soft muck beside a glacial creek. Although I did not see the bear, I knew it was nearby. Those tracks changed the country immediately for me. From that moment on, it was the land of Lewis and Clark, the land of the mountain men of the last century, a valley of the Old West.

The river ahead narrowed down to where two points of timber came out from either bank, and as I approached, I sensed instinctively the possibilities of attack. I was familiar with the wolf lore of the Old World, the packs on the steppes of Russia, the invasion of farms and villages, and had I believed the lurid tales of our early settlers and explorers, I might have been afraid. To the best of my knowledge, however, including the files of the U.S. Fish and Wildlife Service, there has never been a single authenticated instance of unprovoked attack on man.

But still there was a feeling of uneasiness and apprehension, and I knew that if the animals were concerned with anything but satisfying their curiosity, the narrows would be the place for a kill. A swift rush from both points at the same time, a short, unequal scuffle in the snow, and it would be all over. My bones would go down with the ice in the spring, and no one would ever hear the story and no one would be able to explain.

As I neared the points of spruce, I sensed the crash of heavy bodies against the windfalls and brush. Weighing 100, even as much as 120 pounds or more, timber wolves are huge and powerful, can bring down a caribou or a moose, have nothing to fear on the entire continent but man. This was not the first time I had felt they were playing their game of hide-and-seek with me. On other lone midwinter expeditions I had sensed they were close—a hunch perhaps, but as instinctive a reaction when in their immediate range as though I had actually seen them. As I hiked along that night, I knew I was being watched, a lone dark spot moving slowly along the frozen river.

That very morning I had seen where they had pulled down an old buck on the ice of a little lake, and how they had run the deer to exhaustion, sliced at his hamstrings, flanks, his throat; seen the long crimson spurt where they had ripped the jugular, the bits of mangled hide on the snow. He had been large and his horns were broad and palmate, but in the trampled, bloody circle where he had made his last stand he had not lasted long. He might have died slowly of starvation or disease, but he died as he should when his time had come, fighting for his life against his age-old enemies, like the valiant warrior he was out on the open ice.

The wolves had not eaten much, only the entrails and the viscera, but they would return, I knew, to satisfy themselves again. Such was the habit of their kind until we interfered with poison and trap and taught them caution and fear. When that happened, they learned to leave the carcasses after the first feeding and killed more than they would have normally. That kill was part of the age-old cycle of dependency between the wolves and the deer. The predators, by the elimination of the old, the weak, and the diseased, improved the character of the herd and kept the younger and more virile breeding stock alert and aware of danger. The deer provided food when there was no other source, when the heavy snows hid the small rodents, frogs and snakes, grubs and berries and birds that gave the wolves sustenance during all other seasons of the year. There on the ice was evidence of the completed cycle, and though all kills are gruesome things, I was glad to see it, for it meant a wilderness in balance, a primitive country that as yet had not been tamed.

Once I saw a kill being made. I was paddling down the Basswood River on the way to Crooked Lake when I saw a deer running leisurely along a barren, rocky slope paralleling the river. To my surprise a wolf loped behind it, keeping a distance of some thirty yards from its prey. It moved without effort, drifting along like a shadow, then suddenly dashed forward, closed the gap, and with a movement as though in slow motion caught the deer by its nose. The stricken animal turned a somersault and struck the ledge, breaking its back. Instantly the wolf was upon it and the struggle over. I turned toward shore, jumped into the shallows, and ran up the slope to the dead animal, an old doe. The wolf circled warily and once I had a glimpse of it.

I remembered this as I approached the narrows where the spruces stood tall and black against the sky. The shores now were only a stone's throw apart. I must walk straight down the center, must not run nor break my pace. I was suddenly aware that, in spite of reason and my knowledge of the predators, ancient reactions were coming to the fore, intuitive warnings out of the past. Regardless of what I knew, I was responding to an imagined threat like a Stone Age hunter cut off from his cave.

Far ahead, far beyond the dangerous points, two shadows broke from cover and headed directly down the river toward me. I stopped, slipped off my pack, and waited. Nearer and nearer they came, running with the easy, loose-jointed grace that only the big timber wolves seem to have. A hundred yards away they stopped and tried to get my wind; they wove back and forth, swaying as they ran. Then, about fifty feet away they stopped and looked me over. In the moonlight their gray hides glistened and I could see the greenish glint of their eyes. Not a movement or a sound. We stood watching each other as though such meetings were expected and commonplace.

As suddenly as they had appeared, they whirled and were off down the river, two drifting forms against the ice. Never before had I been that close, possibly never again would I see the glint in timber wolves' eyes or have such a chance to study their free and fluid movement. Once more came the long howl, this time far back from the river, and then I heard them no more.

A little later I pushed open the door of an old trapper's cabin I sometimes used and touched a match to the waiting tinder in the stove. As I sat there listening to the roar of it and stowing away my gear, I realized fully what I had seen and what I had felt. Had it not been so cold, I would have left the door opened wide so as not to lose the spell of the moonlit river and the pack ranging its shores.

After I was warmed through and had eaten my supper, I stepped outside. The river was still aglisten, and the far shore looked black and somber. An owl hooted back in the spruce, and I knew what that meant in the moonlit glades. A tree cracked sharply with the frost, and then it was still, so still I could hear the beating of my heart. At last I caught what I was listening for—the long-drawn quavering howl from over the hills, a sound as wild and indigenous to the north as the muskegs or the northern lights.

Although thrilled to hear them, I was saddened when I thought of the constant war of extermination that goes on all over the continent. Practically gone from the United States, wolves are now common only in the Quetico-Superior country, in Canada, and in Alaska, and I knew the day might come when, because of man's ignorance, the great grays would be gone even from there. Just before leaving on my trip up the river I had seen a news story about the killing of six timber wolves by airplane hunters in the Rainy Lake country. The picture showed them strung up on the wing of the plane and the hunters proudly posed beside them. As I studied that picture and the applauding captions, I wondered if the day would ever come when we would understand the importance of wolves.

Knowing the nature of our traditions of the old frontier and the pioneer complex that still guides our attitudes toward wildlife, I realized this might never happen. We do not understand today that we can enjoy the wilderness without fear, still do not appreciate the part predators play in the balanced ecology of any natural community. We seem to prefer herds of semi-domesticated deer and elk and moose, swarms of small game with their natural alertness gone. It is as though we were interested in conserving only a meat supply and nothing of the semblance of the wild.

If the great, gray timber wolves ever leave the Quetico-Superior, the land will lose its character. It may still be a wilderness, but one with the savor and uniqueness gone.

Traveling through such an artificially managed area would be like seeing a cultivated estate with game no longer alert to danger. The ancient biological stability would be destroyed in favor of a tame and colorless substitute.

It was cold, bitterly cold. I hurried back into the cabin and crawled into my sleeping-bag in the corner bunk. Beside me was my pack, and in a pocket my brush-worn copy of Thoreau. I took it out, thumbed through it by the light of the candle. "We need," he said, "to witness our own limits transgressed and some life pasturing freely where we never wander."

The River

I took the trail to the river because I wanted to see open water again after nothing but solid ice on the lakes, brittle frozen brush, and snow that felt like sand. I wanted to see something moving and alive and listen to the gurgle of water as it rippled its way around the rocks of some place that had never quite closed. I knew of such a place, where in the summertime a rapids whitened the blue of the South Kawishiwi.

The snow was unbroken, and the jackpines were so heavily laden that their branches touched the ground. Not a sign of life anywhere until I approached the river and saw the delicate twin tracks of a weasel weaving in and out of the underbrush. The tracks disappeared at the base of a protruding stub—gateway, I knew, to the jungle of grass and duff underneath and the meadow mice that lived there. Then for twenty feet there was no sign until the tracks emerged through a tiny hole in the snow and continued on in a straight line to the open water.

I skied to the very edge of the riffle and stood there, feasting my eyes and ears. Moving water after thirty or forty below, when the whole world had seemed a frozen crystal of blue and white, was an exciting thing. The river was alive and everything within it was alive. Bronze nuggets of gravel moved in the sunlight, and among them danced iridescent bits of shell, whirling madly for a moment only to settle and dance again. Sand eddied impatiently around the larger rocks, and as I watched I knew that, while all life now seemed dead beneath the surface, nothing had really changed. The river moved, and the endless cycle went on as before.

Now I caught an undertone beneath the gurgle of flowing water, the constant *swish-swish* of drifting ice and snow from the mass that was crowding the pool from above in a vain attempt to close the open blue wound in that vast unbroken surface of white. Some night at forty below the ice might win, and there would be no open riffle until spring.

It was then I saw the weasel standing on a log just below me. Snakelike in shape, this tiny bit of venom was less than a foot in length. Totally white with a faint tinge of yellow, the only contrast the jet-black tip of its tail and its beady eyes, the little animal watched me intently. It ran out to the end of the log extending into the water and stood there with one foot uplifted as though wondering whether to plunge in and make it to the other side or retrace its steps and face me.

I sucked softly on the back of my hand, making a sound like the squeak of a meadow mouse. Instantly it turned and looked at me long and steadily, a picture of perfect control and poise. Again I squeaked. Throwing caution to the winds, the weasel dove off the end of the log and in a moment was circling the place where I stood.

How impossible for any small creature to escape such speed and fluid grace, how hopeless to try and run from those smoothly rippling muscles, those sharp black eyes! Suddenly the weasel popped out from under a windfall within a foot of the end of my skis and gave me a wholly malevolent look as though knowing of my deception; then in a flash it was speeding down a fresh rabbit runway through the alders.

Mustela cicognani, the little killer, afraid of nothing ten times its size. I had once seen one attach itself to the throat of a partridge and hang on, biting and chewing through feathers and skin, while the bird climbed high above the trees. I saw the doomed bird plummet to the snow with the weasel still holding on, and while it drank its fill of the hot blood, it defied me. In it was the spirit of all predators, the epitome of speed and grace, deadly concentration, and an audacity born of the instinctive knowledge that there were no enemies to fear. There is poetry in the way a weasel can flow through a maze of branches and grass, in the liquid movement, the perfect control that enables it to live off those less agile than itself.

Ermine, the mark of royalty: white pelts dotted with black tail tips, for centuries the hallmark of those who ruled. How thrilling my boyhood trap lines, the excitement of coming to a set and finding there a tiny frozen form! No compassion then, no feeling of sympathy for the hurt and suffering I had caused; merely wonder at having taken something so beautiful. What pure delight to feel the soft fur! I used to fondle the skins, knew the history of each and every one, became so attached to them that I actually hated to sell them at the end of the season. Far more than the actual worth of the fur on the market was what they meant to me. When I touched those wild furs I somehow made contact with a life that had nothing to do with home or school or parents. I was in a world of my own, a free and beautiful world where all was fantasy and adventure. The trapping made me akin to the creatures I pursued, part of the wilderness world to which they belonged. If anyone had accused me then of doing wrong to the animals I loved, I would not have understood. The magic of that boyhood world did not encompass understanding.

The weasel did not return, so I left the open water and started up the river. I had not gone more than a mile before I found otter tracks. Two of them had been running and slid-

ing over the smooth surface of the river for all the world
like a couple of boys on clear ice. Otters love to play, and in
their traveling wherever there is a chance, be it ice or snow
or slippery mud, they indulge themselves.

I saw a family of them last summer on Robinson Lake in
the Quetico just north of the border. We were trying to catch
a pike off the cliff where the little creek from McIntyre comes
down from the north. A little strip of sandy beach and a
beaver house backed by a jungle of alder and willow and
marsh grass: this was the setting. Although we were several
hundred yards away when we first saw them, the violent
splashing and diving off the beach told us what they were. In
the wilds one can never mistake an otter group at play, their
slipping in and out of the water, their seal-like antics.

On the chance of getting a better view, we paddled over
to the beach and got out. In the wet sand we saw the tracks
of the splayed, webbed feet that make the otter the swiftest-
swimming mammal in the whole north country. Able to
overtake a trout, they are as much at home in the water as
on land.

We got into the canoe again and paddled along the shore,
watching the great protruding shelves of rock, the granite
boulders, the water itself, but not a sign of otters did we see.
We decided they must have gone back up the creek at the
first flash of our paddles.

Then, just as we were rounding a rocky point with a flat
surface jutting out over the water, we spotted three of them
in full view rolling around and playing on the shelf. Surprised, we froze instantly and sat there within twenty feet
of them, moving neither paddles nor eyes. The rock surface
was covered with rough lichens, and the animals rolled upon
it, stretched and scratched themselves, their bellies, their
sides and backs. I could not help thinking of seals as I
watched them, or sea otters—the smooth, almost boneless
appearance of their bodies, the loose skins, the stiffly whisk-
ered doglike faces. Never before in a lifetime of roaming the
woods had I ever been so close.

The canoe drifted toward the rock—fifteen feet, ten, five—
but not until the gunwale almost touched did they become

aware. A moment of petrified realization, a swift plunge into the water, and they were gone. Then, to our amazement they emerged on the other side of the canoe, treading water as only otters can, and looked us over boldly while they snorted and blew their nostrils clear. Up and down they bobbed like three anchored posts, at times seeming to emerge almost entirely out of the water.

Their curiosity satisfied, they swam around the canoe and headed down along the shore the way they had come. A far larger head appeared out in the open lake — the mother otter, blowing and whistling, warning her foolhardy young. We followed the family back to the beach, watching them diving and playing as though they had nothing to fear. They romped on the sand for a while and finally disappeared up the creek. *Lutra canadensis* is one of the most beautiful animals in the north and is blessed with the most spirit and personality.

Although a killer like its little cousin the ermine, it is somehow different. Surely, like the rest it must kill to live, but when I see otters at play I feel that the killing must be almost incidental, that it is done in a spirit of play rather than to satisfy an implacable lust for blood.

Once I saw a mother otter with her young watching a tight little raft of half-grown mergansers coasting off the shore. They, too, were treading water, but I was not so close this time as I would have liked to be. I could see them plainly, however, and as yet they had not seen the canoe. Then the mother dove toward the unsuspecting raft of ducklings. A pause and one of them disappeared. A moment later she came ashore and gave the carcass to her young. Three different times this performance was repeated before the merganser took its little flock out of danger. To otters life is never dull.

Toward midafternoon I saw the track of a lone fisher, *Martes pennanti*, the Pekan of the Indians. Its track crossed the river and headed into a cedar swamp, and, had I been an Indian, I would have followed it, sure that eventually the animal would climb a tree. A trapper told me once that he had often stayed with a trail for days at a time and had almost always been successful. The fisher, too, is one of the *Mus-*

telidae but looks more like a stocky cat then the others, more like a small edition of the dreaded wolverine than the otter or the ermine. Equally at home in the trees or on the ground, it seems to prefer a range near running water. One of the few predators in the north able to kill a porcupine and live, it has learned to turn the animal over on its back or disembowel it in a tree. Until recent years, the fisher's rarity was one of the reasons porcupines became more numerous, for with their chief enemy gone there was nothing to fear.

I have seen only three live fishers in my life. Once, just after the first snow came I saw one standing in plain view on a windfall not thirty feet away. In the dusk it looked black, though I knew its fur was grizzled tawny brown. It stood there and watched me and then slid off into the underbrush for all the world like a large cat on the prowl.

Once, while exploring the rugged country between Robinson and Brent lakes I was resting on the edge of a cliff overlooking a rough talus slope below me. As I sat there above the valley I heard a sound, a scratching on bark. Thinking it might be a red squirrel, I looked up, and there, crouched on a branch of a gnarled Norway pine not ten feet above, were two fishers watching me. I did not move, nor did they, and we sat there for some time staring at each other. Then, without warning, the animals leaped recklessly over the cliff to the jagged talus slope below. I was horrified, thinking that surely they would cripple themselves, but they bounded down unhurt into the birch and aspen of the valley. Only fishers could have done what they did then, only animals with perfect balance and control.

I have a strong attachment for all of the *Mustelidae*, from the tiny ermine to the wolverine. Each is different, each a distinct personality. To be sure, the ecological factors are important—the endless cycle of carnivores and herbivores, the inevitable assimilation of vegetable matter to flesh and blood and back again. Part of the ancient cycle, one form of life cannot exist without the other, but what really counts is how they contribute to the character and quality of the wilderness.

As I headed back through the woods, the west was flaming and I saw the glow of it through the trees. From a hilltop I could look across miles of purple ridges. The glow faded to lavender and then to mauve, and in between were streaks of orange and apple green. I stood there on the hill and watched until the cold reminded me to move. The temperature was dropping fast and I could feel the swift change; it would be twenty or thirty below by morning. Perhaps the riffle down by the river would close now and there would be no sight or sound of movement the next time I came through.

Dark House

It was just ten years ago that my son Bob came home to catch the feeling of the Minnesota-Ontario border country in mid-winter. He wanted, above all, to sit in a "dark house" with me again and watch the circling decoy and the scene below the ice. He wanted time to think long thoughts and hear the whispering of the snow outside the thin, tarpaper walls. He wanted the good feeling he used to know at night after a long day on skis, and perhaps the taste of a fish fresh from the icy waters of the lakes of the north.

So, one morning in January, though it was twenty below, we took off for the old haunts. The ski harnesses creaked as we pushed across the lower reaches of Fall Lake. Smoke rose straight above the chimneys in the little town of Winton at the end of the road and golden sun dogs* blazed over the horizon. It was far too cold to travel slowly. We pushed hard

*Spots of color, sometimes resembling miniature suns, seen one on either side of the sun when, in very cold weather, it shines through ice crystals in the atmosphere.

on our sticks, and the skis hissed over the powder-dry snow. We were the only ones abroad, the only ones foolish enough to be outside when we did not have to be. Still, fresh deer tracks crossed the lake, and on the portage into Cedar there were signs of rabbits, weasels, and mice.

A tiny tarpaper shack off the end of a long point was our goal. A friend had set it up weeks ago, told us where the spear was cached and the wooden decoy. For its use, we were to bring him a fish. That meant we had to take two. We shoveled the snow away from the door, fanned a flame to life in the little stove, and dug the spear and the decoy out of a drift.

Six inches of ice had to be cut out of the hole. We filled the coffeepot, closed the door, and settled down to wait. Outside the wind howled, but the little shelter was cozy and warm. At first we could see nothing but the green translucent water, but gradually our vision cleared and we could see farther and farther into the depths, finally to the very bottom itself. Light streamed through the snow and ice, and the bottom all but glowed.

In our field of vision were several whitish rocks and bits of shell, important landmarks of the scene. Soon eel grass and feathery milfoil emerged in the half-light, weaving slowly in the slight current of the narrows. The rocks and shells became as familiar as though we had been watching them for weeks, the tufts of waving grass as outstanding as trees in a meadow. In one corner was a clam, its narrow furrow distinct and sharp in the sand. A shaft of light angled over our hunting ground, light reflected through flashing prisms of ice. The stage was set for action. This was worth the cold trek out, compensation for weeks of waiting; it was a scene of stark beauty and suspense such as the most elaborate stage setting has never attained.

The spear rested easily against the inside edge of the ice, its handle free and ready to grasp, a cord fastened to Bob's wrist. Occasionally he shifted the point of a tine before it became too firmly embedded in its notch, twisted it slightly so that when the great moment came there would be no resistance, no wrenching free, nothing to interfere with the thrust. When the time came, the strike must be made with lightning speed.

I played the decoy, a six-inch model of a sucker minnow replete with fins and tail of shining tin. Whittled from a piece of cedar, it was weighted with lead and hung from the end of a string. Its tail was set so that with each motion of my hand it made wide and beautiful circles all around the hole.

As the coffee began to simmer, we shed outer jackets and mitts. Outside, it was still close to twenty below and the snow was whispering as Bob had hoped. After an hour of tension we began to relax, talked quietly about many things. A fish house is a fine place for visiting—not for arguments or weighty ideas, but rather for small talk, local politics and gossip, things we had seen coming in, ideas that required no effort, short simple thoughts that came as easily as breathing. Furthermore, our energies must be conserved for the moment when the flash of a silver side below would eclipse everything else in the world.

"A northern pike will taste pretty good tonight," I said.

"Would taste pretty good" was Bob's reply.

"We'll clean it before it freezes," I said. "Save us the job when we get home."

"See that clam?" said Bob. "It's moving toward the outside of the hole. Getting out of the way while there's time."

"Those deer tracks this morning looked as though they'd been chased. Twenty feet at a jump for a while."

"Heading for the cedar on the south shore, really makin' time."

The small talk went on and on, and after a while there was nothing more to say and we lapsed into quiet, just sat and stared into the hole, watching the rhythmic turns of the little decoy, back and forth, around and around, its metal fins flashing in the light. After a time our vision blended with the bottom itself and we began to feel as though we were a part of the subterranean world below us, part of the clean sand, the white rocks, the waving eel grass. We became intimately familiar with each irregularity of the bottom, the ripple marks, the moving habits of each blade of grass, the air bubbles at the edge of the ice, even the shadows of clouds drifting by outside. Two hours went by and our senses all but fused with the blue-green environment below.

Then, when we had begun to feel as though nothing could ever change, as though we might have been sitting in that same position for years, a huge torpedolike shape slipped swiftly into the open and the static little world we had created exploded before our eyes. The grasses waved erratically, the white rocks disappeared, the water roiled.

The spear! screamed everything within us. Slowly—so slowly—cramped senses became aware, muscles began to move. As in a dream, fingers tightened around the cold, heavy steel; the point, withdrawn from its icy notch, hung poised, ready to strike. Directly below lay the long, dark form of a great northern pike, its fins and tail moving slowly, its gill covers opening and closing with barely perceptible motion.

"Now!" came the shout, and suddenly the spear plunged downward, and in a violent instant the water boiled and the fish, the rocks, and the weeds disappeared in a green-white turmoil of confusion.

The spear and the fish came out of the hole in a cascade of water. I pushed out the door and we stumbled outside into the brilliant dazzle of sunlight on the snow, shouting, laughing at our good fortune, pounding each other on the back. This was a pinnacle of experience, and during that instant it seemed that few triumphs in the world of men could compare with it.

The pike stopped its thrashing at last and began to stiffen in the cold. We stepped back through the little door into quiet and darkness once more.

Finally the water cleared, and we could now see fresh scales on the bottom. The eel grass and milfoil were waving once more, and there again were the identical rocks and the whitened bits of shell. Even the clam was in the same position, working its way slowly toward the outside perimeter of our field. It seemed impossible that things could be the same after the violent eruption of a short time ago. But nothing had changed at all—a few more air bubbles under the ice, the scattered scales on the sand. Again the rhythmic turns of the decoy, around and around and around, its silver fins flashing in the light. The spear point wore itself down into another icy notch.

"That's one," said Bob. "That one goes to the house."

"The next one is ours," I answered, "the one we'll clean for supper."

Again the scene became familiar, and soon we were finished talking, just sitting there watching and waiting as men have watched and waited since the beginning of time. The drifting snow whispered and swirled around our little house.

A shadow crossed one corner and the waving grasses trembled slightly, bowed gently toward the movement, came back to their old positions. The spear was loosened from its notch. At that moment the whole civilized world moved back to where it belonged, faded into a background that was nothing compared to the tremendous event taking place before our eyes. The grasses trembled as though expecting something to happen. The water itself seemed charged.

Then the shadow returned and another pike lay directly below us, so close and real our numbed senses could not grasp what had actually happened. Its fins were moving slowly, its gills opening and closing. It lay there quietly looking at the decoy quivering at the end of its string.

The spear was withdrawn and with a single movement plunged into the water. Again the white-and-green turmoil, the open door and the sunshine.

We had enough: one for the house and one for our supper. We cached the spear and decoy, closed the door, and started off for home. It was a little warmer now and the skis slid smoothly over the trail we had made that morning. The west was orange and mauve and apple green, and the birches shone silver in the last level rays of the sun. By the time we reached the portage it was dusk and the afterglow burned behind the black masses of pine and spruce.

When we reached Fall Lake we could see the lights of the village at the end of the bay. Smoke still rose straight above the chimneys. With the dark it would be twenty below again, and in the morning the sun dogs would be out. The ice would soon be thick over the hole we had cut, and the tar-paper shack would be cold and dark. The grasses would tremble on the bottom, and the clam would plow its furrow unseen and undisturbed.

The Spawning

It was February and the mercury was below zero. A woodsman friend and I took off from the cabin when the moon was high and the surface of the lake glittering in its shine. The snow was firm, and the skis hissed as we pushed along. We did not stop to look at the moon or the stars, but were conscious only of the fact we were moving through a brittle icy brightness, that the stars were close, almost near enough to touch. It was one of those winter nights in the north, one of those times close to midnight that come only when it is still and the moon is full.

We were off on important business, far more important

than just going for a ski or enjoying the night. We were out to watch a spawning in midwinter, the mating of the eelpout, those brown eel-like deep-water fish that thrive in the cold depths of northern lakes. Seldom is one ever taken by hook and line except when they approach the shallows and the rivers to spawn, and rarely is one seen during the warm months of the year because of the deeps they frequent. Only in midwinter can their strange primordial mating be observed.

The river mouth was a mile away, opening like a lighted hallway into the black embankment of hills to the south. Beyond its far door were the rapids, a place where the frozen highway of the river was still alive and moving over the rocks. We stopped at the mouth and listened, and there was the same murmuring we had heard the first night we slept on the point, a murmuring that seemed to blend with our breathing and with the pounding of our hearts.

The eelpout need shallow water, moving water full of oxygen, gravel, and sand, to mix the sperm with the eggs, to keep them rolling over and over until the first cell divisions take place. As we skied up the narrowing river, its sound became plainer and there was a distinct and steady rushing. The rocky shores drew together, then seemed to merge and become part of the woods. Now before us the rapids were suddenly loud and clear and we saw the glint of them in the moonlight.

We stopped, unstrapped our skis, and went into the trees, stayed quiet until the cold made us move. No vibration of the bank, no breaking twigs must announce our coming. Not until we were within ten feet of the rapids did we shine our lights and then saw such a sight as is seldom glimpsed by modern man: a struggling, squirming mass of fish, the brownish snakelike bodies with their sinuous dorsal fins the full length of them twisted around each other, the entire contorted mass turning over and over, churning the water into froth.

Fascinated and oblivious of the cold, we stood and watched, for this was a scene out of the dim past, this mating, the rapids white with the concentration of eggs and milt and the foam from the thrashing fish. Over and over rolled the mass, churning the precious eggs and sperms with the liveness of their bodies, whipping them together so there was no chance of an egg not meeting its exploring mate. Out of the depths they had come, swimming into the river and beneath the ice to reach this stretch of open water in the rapids and here in the night exchange their offerings.

But why in February, when the elements seemed against the success of any mating? Why not during the warm days of spring or in the summer or fall, when all other species spawned? Why this terrible urge to leave the deeps in the dead of winter and spawn at night? Why does the whisky-jack lay its eggs during the winter and hatch its young during the bitter days of March? Why does the horned owl do the same? Why do some species violate all traditional procedure? Such thoughts ran through my mind as we watched the eelpout spawn.

To answer, one must go back to the beginnings of time and find out why these creatures obey urges that today seem beyond reason, urges that were implanted in their genetic structure long before they came to present environments. In the case of the eelpout, a relative of the salt-water cod, it may have been that eons ago it was trapped in the north when the sea that brought it in finally retreated. Perhaps it came in the arm of the sea that laid down the iron deposits of the Mesabi, perhaps from one of the great extensions of glacial waters from the north. Whatever the cause of its introduction, somehow the species managed to survive, adapted itself gradually to the lack of salinity and the shallower depths of inland lakes, changed its habits of feeding and migration; instead of spawning on the ocean reefs it once frequented, it found it could survive by using open streams and the shallows of the lakes. It still keeps the ancient schedule, however, and spawns when the cod spawns in the sea, adhering that much to the age-old habits of the race.

The fish gradually became quiet and the brown eel-like shapes slipped away into the calmer waters below the riffle. There we could see them lying in the shadows, fanning the water with their long, finned tails, waiting lazily until the strange apparitions and the unwelcome lights should go away. This was a vital task that brooked no interruption, far more important than feeding or any other activity. As with all species, the eelpout's entire life history led up to this supreme event. It was the climax of existence, the ultimate biological experience toward which everything previous was merely a preparation. When the crucial time was at hand, nothing must ever interfere for long. Like the trout, the salmon, and the eel, these fish had come from the depths to spawn where they themselves had first known the quickening of life. Each year for untold centuries the eelpout had come out of the lake to this particular place and at this very time. Each female left up to half a million or more of some of the smallest eggs produced by fish of inland waters. No wonder the rapids were colored by their release.

The turbulence had ceased and the fish lay furtively in the pool below. We had stopped them in the midst of their ritual, but they would begin again as soon as we were gone. A few nights more and they would swim back into the depths to wait another year before the urge took hold of them again. It was bitterly cold and we had been there for most of an hour. We dropped the flashlights into the pack, strapped on the skis, and pushed back on our trail to the open lake.

While hurrying across the moonlit ice, I could not erase from my mind what we had seen, something that might have taken place in a pool millions of years before. Here was life obeying the urge to reproduce, disregarding all else, bent only on fulfilling the ever implacable law of procreation. For sheer primeval savagery, nothing I had ever seen compared to this. It seemed unreal as the river mouth grew dim behind us and the point ahead lay white and frosty under the moon. I felt somewhat uneasy, as though I had witnessed something I wasn't supposed to see, as though for a guilty moment I had peeked under the curtain at sheer brutality stripped of any of the beauty and joy and delight that is associated with the mating of the animals and birds I knew. Somehow it was as though I had done the unpardonable, stolen a look far back into the dim beginnings of life, when forms on earth today were still eons from their origins.

We stopped at the end of the point and listened. We were warm now and our breath was frozen fog. After we were quiet awhile we heard again the soft whisper of the rapids. The eelpout were back at their work, rolling over and over once more, twined around each other, slithering and slipping from one entangled group to another, beating the water white with their milt and eggs.

Perhaps it was the shape of the fish that affected me, the sinuous twisting forms reminding me of a nest of snakes I once had seen, a quivering mass of vipers. But even more was the feeling that I had watched some prehistoric scene, something from the age of fishes, long before reptilian monsters ruled the earth, long before birds and mammals began their slow climb out of the primordial ooze. It was a strangely uncomfortable realization, and I almost wished I had not gone.

The mating of birds is a different thing, the pleasant happy nesting days of robins and bluebirds, of ducks and sparrows. There, courtship means song and brilliant coloring and devotion of one mate to another. All mating until now had seemed a happy thing, but this was entirely different. Here was deadly seriousness, or so it seemed to me, a seriousness without music, romance, or joy, a powerful urge born of a force as inexorable as the turning of the spheres.

I felt much the same in the seal caves on the Oregon coast. It seemed then, too, as though I were looking far back into time at a scene that men had long forgotten. As I listened to the all-engulfing rush of the surf through the cave entrances and the roaring and barking of hundreds of seals, a sound magnified a thousand times by the cavern walls, I knew this was such a sound as ruled the earth long before the coming of man. I thought as I looked down the dim reaches of those cliff caves that nothing had changed there for millions of years and the traffic on the highway just above was but a temporary thing. That night too I was disturbed vaguely, for again I had lifted the veil and glimpsed the hidden past.

Another time, in the Florida Everglades, I listened to the rasping cough of alligators and the night-screaming of countless birds, and as I lay there in the great swamp I was back in the primeval. That night the old hidden fears were with me, fears of the unknown that had lain deeply hidden in my subconscious.

We started a fire back on the beach, a great roaring fire, and threw on driftwood logs of cedar and pine. We sat before the blaze and toasted ourselves while the moonlight grew dim and the sparks flew high. There before the fire, what I had seen seemed not as awesome as before. Surely it was a glimpse into the past, but this I also knew: that out of that midnight breeding, out of the roaring seal caves of Oregon, and the sounds of the reptilian era down in the Glades had come all of the life we know, all of the beauty we now take for granted, all of the song and gladness, as well as the mind of man, who could look at such things and give them meaning.

The next morning I sat in the sunlight in front of the cabin and listened to the merry song of the chickadees, even though it was all of thirty below zero. I watched a red squirrel climb a jackpine to look for cones and then run around over the snow to find some it had cached. It was a bright, sunlit, frozen world again and the spawning, while it still went on, seemed not as desperate as before.

The coffeepot was on in the fireplace, and wood smoke curled up into the still morning air. Sun dogs shone over the hills back of the beach, and trees cracked loudly with the frost. It was no time to be sitting outside, even in the sun. This was a morning for reading and inviting one's soul. Later, when the crust was warmed, I might ski to a hole off one of the islands and try for a trout.

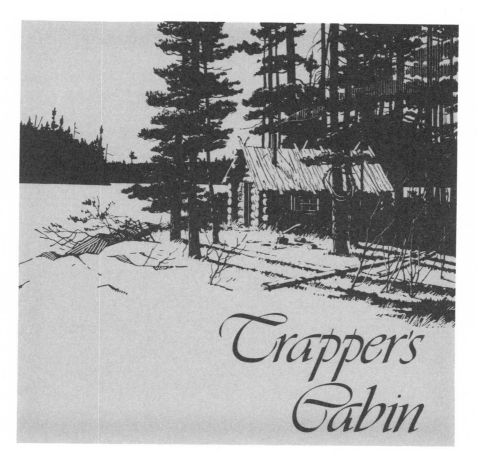

Trapper's Cabin

The cabin on Snowbank Lake was primitive; the unpeeled logs were chinked with moss; there was no floor and only one small window. The little shelter faded into the tall, black spruces around it as if it had always been there. It smelled of balsam, for in one corner was a bunk full of the resinous tips and on the packed-dirt floor needles were the pattern.

The cabin had not been built for summer comfort or view. It had no real-estate value. It had one purpose only: to provide comfort at the end of a long day on the trap lines, shelter from the gales of winter when the snow was deep and the cold enough to sear a man's lungs.

Even for a trapper's cabin it was small, just big enough for a man and his outfit, a tiny stove, a corner table, and the bunk; there were hand-whittled pegs for clothes and packs, a narrow shelf below the window. But at night, when the trees cracked with frost and the bitter wind whipped the unprotected shore, it was cozy and warm as a bear's den under a windfall. The roof was low, and the rafters stuck far out from the eaves as though the builder had forgotten to trim them. Those eaves gave the cabin the effect of squatting low beneath the trees, and made it as much a part of the forest floor as a moss-covered boulder or a hummock cushioned with duff. Only a few spruce nearby had been cut for the logs, and with the passing years the little gap had been filled with new growth until there seemed to be no perceptible break between the roof and the low-hanging branches of the trees.

When I entered that cabin I felt as Thoreau did when he said, "Drive life into a corner and reduce it to its simplest terms." Here, if anywhere, was the simplicity he meant. This was no place for fancy or unnecessary equipment. The cabin meant moccasins, rough wool, and leather—and simple thoughts. The complicated problems of society, politics, war and peace seemed far removed. The only thoughts that thrived here were of squirrels and birds and snowshoe trails. Here I felt as much a part of the out-of-doors as when sleeping under a ledge.

I liked to lie in the balsam bunk and look up at the pole rafters and study the deer-mouse nest in one corner and the lichen and fungi that had taken hold on the rough logs. As the cabin became warm, the mouse thawed out; a slight rustling, and suddenly big transparent ears and bright black eyes emerged from the nest. For a long time the little animal would watch me, and when convinced I was harmless would come down to the table to pick up crumbs.

Sometimes a red squirrel came in through a hole under the eaves. Again the long contemplation and final acceptance. He and I were partners, in a sense—my part to leave something on the table, his to make me feel I belonged.

Sometimes at night I would waken and listen to the tips of the spruce branches rubbing against the walls, caressing them softly. That cabin was of the living forest, and would eventually be moss and duff again. At such times my thoughts merged with the trees and the sound of their movement in the wind, their creaking and moaning as they rubbed against one another. The cabin satisfied a longing for closeness to a natural environment, the hunger to return for a little while to the wilderness. Centuries of caves, of shelters under the trees, of dry spots beneath ledges and windfalls, of listening to the sounds of the night have left their mark.

Another cabin that gave me this feeling was on the Sand River south of my home. It, too, was of logs, but roofed with wide strips of birchbark anchored with stones. The rafters were wide enough in their overlap to shelter a woodpile underneath, an ax, a saw, and other gear, generous enough to heal the break between the walls and the ground. The cabin made a picture squatting there on its little spit of land, commanding a view up and down the river. On one side spruces and balsams hedged it closely, but the other side was snuggled close against a great gray rock out of reach of the wind. The trapper who built it may have thought it was just another shelter, but, far more than that, it was a picture in logs and rock that gave pleasure to all who passed. He was probably more of an artist than he knew, unable to resist the view up and down the river, the sunrises and sunsets, and the sound of whistling wings as mallards flew over on their way to the rice beds beyond.

Charley Laney's Stony River cabin was surrounded by high hills, but you could hear the whisper of the river as it flowed across the boulders down below. Here was isolation in a wild and glorious setting. It reminded me of cabins in the Austrian Tyrol, little shelters perched on inaccessible crags reached only by steep mountain trails. There were no sunsets because the dusk settled swiftly between the hills, no vistas, no sense of space—as wild and lonely a place as the bottom of a canyon, and Charley Laney, the mad trapper who built it, found there a mystery that complemented his own nature. I sometimes wondered how mad he was— whether he was not saner than many who passed judgment upon him. He loved to sit on his stoop and play his violin to the accompaniment of the rapids. He was as much a part of his setting as the Sibelius he loved was part of the forests and lakes of Finland.

There are many such cabins in the north, and many mansions called cabins. Most are comfortable and beautiful in their way, but when I enter there is no change for me, merely an extension of civilized living away from the towns. Motorboats, highways, and planes make them as accessible as suburban homes. I find no sense of seclusion or solitude in them, for their conveniences carry the associations and responsibilities of urban living. Sometimes they are so comfortable, so removed from all physical effort, that they nullify the real purpose of going to the woods: doing things in primitive ways and recapturing simplicity.

Trappers' cabins are as natural as tents or tepees. They belong to solitude and wilderness as do the trees and rocks themselves. In them the wilderness always sings. Each time that deer mouse came to feed, I caught a single elfin note. I heard it on the Sand River one stormy night, when the drifting snow was full of the sound of wings; and on the Stony, when Charley's violin blended with the music of the rapids so closely I could not tell them apart and knew he was feeling not only the scene around him, but the hinterlands of Europe's north.

Wilderness Music

One night I followed a ski trail into the Lucky Boy Valley. It was dark and still, and the pines and spruces there almost met overhead. During the day it had snowed, and the festooned trees were vague, massed drifts against the stars. Breathless after my run, I stopped to rest and listen. In that snow-cushioned place there was no sound, no wind moaning in the branches, no life or movement of any kind. Leaning on my sticks, I thought of Jack Linklater, a Scotch-Cree of the Hudson's Bay Company. In such a place he would have heard the music, for he had a feeling for the "wee" people and for many things others did not understand. Sometimes when we were on the trail together he would ask me to listen, and when I could not hear he would laugh. Once, in a stand of quaking aspen in a high place, when the air was full of their whispering, he dropped his pack and a strange, happy light was in his eyes. Another time, during the harvesting of wild rice, when the dusk was redolent with the parching fires on the shores of Hula Lake, he called me to him, for he felt that somehow I must hear the music too.

"Can't you hear it now?" he said. "It's very plain tonight."

I listened, but heard nothing, and as I watched the amused and somewhat disappointed look on his face I wondered if he were playing a game with me. That time he insisted he could hear the sound of women's and children's voices and the high quaver of an Indian song, though we were far from the encampment. Now that the years have passed and Jack has gone to the Happy Hunting Grounds, I believe that he actually heard something and the reason I could not was that this was music for Indians and for those whose ears were attuned.

One night we were camped on the Maligne River in the Quetico on a portage trail used for centuries by Indians and *voyageurs*. The moon was full, and the bowl below the falls was silver with mist. As we sat listening to the roar of Twin Falls, there seemed to be a sound of voices of a large party making the carry. The sound ebbed and swelled in volume with the ebb and flow of the plunging water. That night I thought I heard them too, and Jack was pleased. Wilderness music? Imagination? I may never know, but this much I do know from traveling with Jack: he actually heard something, and those who have lived close to nature all of their lives are sensitive to many things lost to those in the cities.

We send out costly expeditions to record the feelings, expressions, and customs of primitive tribes untouched by civilization, considering such anthropological research to be worthwhile because it gives us an inkling of why we moderns behave as we do. We recognize that a great deal has been lost to us during the so-called civilized centuries — intuitive awarenesses that primitives still possess.

While most of us are too far removed to hear the wilderness music that Jack Linklater heard, there are other forms, not so subtle, perhaps, but still capable of bringing to our consciousness the same feelings that have stirred human-kind since the beginning of time. Who is not stirred when the wild geese go by, when the coyotes howl on a moonlit night, or when the surf crashes against the cliffs? Such sounds have deep appeal because they are associated with the background of the race. Why does the rhythmic tom-tom beat of drums affect us? Because it, too, is primitive and was part of our heritage centuries before music as we know it now was conceived. Wilderness music to me is any sound that brings to mind the wild places I have known.

Once during a long absence from the north I heard the call of a loon, the long, rollicking laughter that in the past I had heard echoing across the wild reaches of the Quetico lakes. It was in Tennessee that I heard it, but the instant I caught the first long wail, chills of gladness chased themselves up and down my spine. For a long time I stood there and listened, but I did not hear it again. While I waited, the north came back to me with a rush and visions of wilderness lakes and rivers crowded upon me. I saw the great birds flying into the sunsets, groups of them playing over the waters of Lac la Croix, Kawnipi, and Batchewaung. I saw the reaches of Saganaga in the early morning, a camp on some lonely island with the day's work done and nothing to do but listen and dream. And then in the recesses of my mind the real calling began as it had a thousand times in the past, the faintest hint of an echo from over the hills, answered before it died by a closer call and that in turn by another until the calling of the loons from all the lakes around blended in a continuous symphony.

There were other times that also came back to me: times when the clouds were dark and the waves rolling high, when the calling reached a pitch of madness that told of coming storm; mornings when the sun was bright and happy laugh-ter came from the open water; nights when one lone call embodied all the misery and tragedy in the world. I knew when once a man had known that wild and eery calling and lost himself in its beauty, should he ever hear a hint of it again, no matter where he happened to be, he would have a vision of the distance and freedom of the north.

One day in the south of England I was walking through a great beech wood on an old estate near Shrivenham. There was a little brook flowing through the woods, and its gurgle as it ran through a rocky dell seemed to accentuate my sense of the age of those magnificent trees. I was far from home, as far away from the wilderness of the north as I had ever been. Those great trees were comforting to me even though I knew that just beyond them was open countryside.

Then suddenly I heard a sound that changed everything: a soft, nasal twang from high in the branches, the call of a nuthatch. Instantly that beech grove was transformed into a stand of tall, stately pines; the brown beech leaves on the ground became a smooth carpet of golden needles, and beyond this cared-for forest were rugged ridges and deep, timbered valleys, roaring rivers and placid lakes, with a smell of resin and duff in the sun. The call of the nuthatch had done all that, had given me a vision of the wilderness as vivid as though for the moment I had actually been there.

How satisfying to me are the sounds of a bog at night! I like to paddle into a swampy bay in the lake country and just sit there and listen to the slow sloshing-around of moose and deer, the sharp pistol crack of a beaver tail slapping the water, the guttural, resonant pumping of a bittern. But the real music of a bog is the frog chorus. If they are in full swing when you approach, they stop by sections as though part of the orchestra was determined to carry on in spite of the faintheartedness of the rest. You must sit quietly for some time before they regain their courage. At first there are individual piping notes, a few scattered guttural croaks, then a confused medley as though the instruments were being tuned. Finally, in a far corner a whole section swings into tremulous music, hesitant at the start but gradually gathering momentum and volume. Soon a closer group begins, and then they all join in until there is again a sustained and grand crescendo of sound.

This is a primeval chorus, the sort of wilderness music that reigned over the earth millions of years ago and floated across the pools of the carboniferous era. One of the most ancient sounds on earth, it is a continuation of music from the past, and, no matter where I listen to a bog at night, strange feelings stir within me.

One night in the south of Germany I was walking along the River Main at Frankfurt. It was spring and sunset. Behind me were the stark ruins of the city, the silhouettes of broken walls and towers, the horrible destruction of the bombing. Across the river was a little village connected with the city by the broken span of a great bridge. In the river were the rusting hulls of barges and sunken boats. The river gurgled softly around them and around the twisted girders of the blown-up span. It was a scene of desolation and sadness.

Then I was conscious of a sound that was not of the war, the hurrying whisper of wings overhead. I turned, and there against the rosy sky was a flock of mallards. I had forgotten that the river was a flyway, that there were still such delightful things as the sound of wings at dusk, rice beds yellowing in the fall, and the soft sound of quacking all through the night. A lone flock of mallards gave all that to me, awoke a thousand memories as wilderness music always does.

There are many types of music, each one different from the rest: a pack of coyotes and the wild, beautiful sound of them as they tune up under the moon; the song of a white-throated sparrow, its one, clear note so closely associated with trout streams that whenever I hear one I see a sunset-tinted pool and feel the water around my boots; the groaning and cracking of ice forming on the lakes; the swish of skis or snowshoes in dry snow—wilderness music, all of it, music for Indians and for those who have ears to hear.

Epilogue

Over a hundred years ago Henry David Thoreau made a strange and prophetic statement: "In wildness is the preservation of the world." He said this while living in his cabin at Walden near the rural village of Concord, at a time when the North American continent was comparatively unsettled and the west still largely unknown.

The Space Age of today is a far cry from the elemental world he knew, and he could not have dreamed what was coming. But he was a reader of signs, had listened to the Pipes of Pan, and had watched what was happening to the minds of men and what they were doing to the land. He was concerned about the future, and when he spoke it was with the wisdom of a seer.

As proof of his vision, we, during the last half-century, have opened up a Pandora's box of treasures and powers that have changed the entire pattern of our lives. Scientific advance has brought a host of developments: nuclear energy, computers, control of disease, the exploration of space. We are probing the secrets of life, the ocean depths, the interior of the earth, and moving so fast we are stunned by our progress.

Sociological change is equally swift with the birth of new countries; a United Nations; world organizations for Health, Agriculture, and Finance; alliances; Common Markets; a multiplicity of international complexities undreamed of even a generation ago.

Air travel and a world-wide communications network are wiping out isolation. New ideologies and religious nostrums are replacing ancient beliefs. We are challenging old moralities, mores, and integrities, and our dependency on all other forms of life. There is no end to the pyramiding of human populations, and as more space is being occupied we grow fearful, as do other creatures, that territory for expansion and food is limited.

Two major world conflicts and a score of lesser ones during this period literally tore us from the relatively peaceful and natural world we had known until then, hurling us into the whirring complexities of the technological era they spawned. The days of the old frontiers ended; a dynamic and exciting millennium lay ahead.

Never before had any people lived in such affluence; and with all the comforts, luxuries, and amenities of the age available to us, happiness and contentment should have been ours. Instead there is tension and strain, frustration and disillusionment, and growing instability. As the tempo increases, the long, slow rhythms of the past are forgotten in the frenzy of our pace. Now, as though to climax our progress, we are embarking on the greatest adventure and possible tragedy of all: exploring the universe while holding in our hands forces that threaten our survival.

As a result of the headlong drive of our technology, the worship of the goal of unlimited expansion of industry, and a madly spiraling gross national product, we face an ecological crisis. We have poisoned air, water, and soil, defiled the land with mountains of garbage, leveled hills, drained marshes and lakes, rerouted rivers; we have violated our countrysides, filled our cities with ugliness and clamor, with natural resources depleted to the point where we see their end.

Appalled at what we have done to our living space, we

believe science has all the answers and the inventive genius which produced our technology can save us from disaster. We refuse to believe that keeping our earth habitable is our greatest challenge. If we fail to reverse the trend we will lose our cherished freedoms and the richness and beauty America once knew.

Aware of the mounting tension and strain, the crowding, confusion, and artificiality, we are beginning to wonder and ask questions. Why is there less laughter in the world, why less time than there used to be, with fewer abiding satisfactions in our hurried, gadget-ridden lives? Is this the good life, the end result of our wealth; and if not, how can we regain some of the joys we seem to have lost?

No one is naïve enough to believe we should abandon our scientific achievements and return to a primitive culture with its brutalities, hazards, and hardships, but we are wondering if we can experience some of the basic rewards of living closer to nature, know again some small sense of oneness and belonging, of silence, open country, and the timelessness our forebears took for granted.

It is not surprising we ask such vital questions, for we cannot forget the recent frontiers or easily erase our long prehistoric background. In spite of urbanity and sophistication, the wilderness and all it means is still part of us. Adaptations take eons of time, and adjustment for man is no swifter than for other forms of life.

The ultimate question is what kind of world we want. To answer, we must ponder the purpose of man, what constitutes the good society, the good life, and possibly the ancient dream. Do we want a world of beauty in which it is pleasant to live, or one becoming increasingly strident, violent, and ugly? Are we willing to forsake some affluence to attain our goal, set new priorities, be content with less in return for a richer and more meaningful life? Are we willing to place spiritual values above the material, live with nature and develop an ecology of man in harmony with all other creatures?

Will we value wisdom more than cleverness and understand what the Sage of Concord really meant when he said,

"In wildness is the preservation of the world"? If we say yes, there is hope for a world of beauty and meaning in which our spiritual roots will ever be nourished by love of the earth.

Guides to the Quetico-Superior country and the Big North

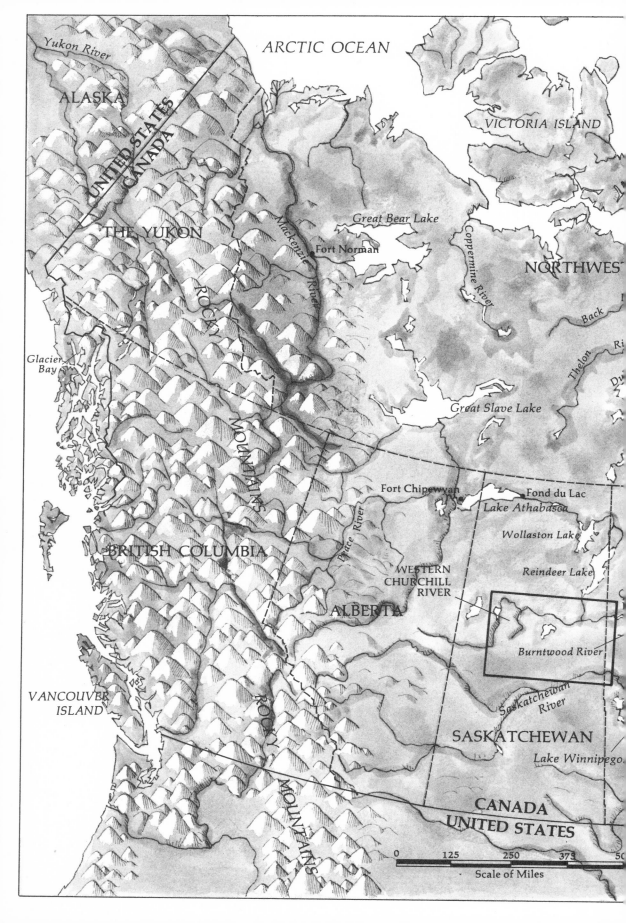

Central and Western Canada

BAFFIN ISLAND

TERRITORIES

Hudson Strait

Chesterfield Inlet

HUDSON BAY

Fort Churchill

York Factory

Nelson River

Hayes River

River

NITOBA

e
peg

Severn River

Winisk River

James Bay

Albany River

Moose River

Abitibi River

ONTARIO

Lake Nipigon

Lake of the Woods

QUETICO-
SUPERIOR

Lake Superior

Rainy River

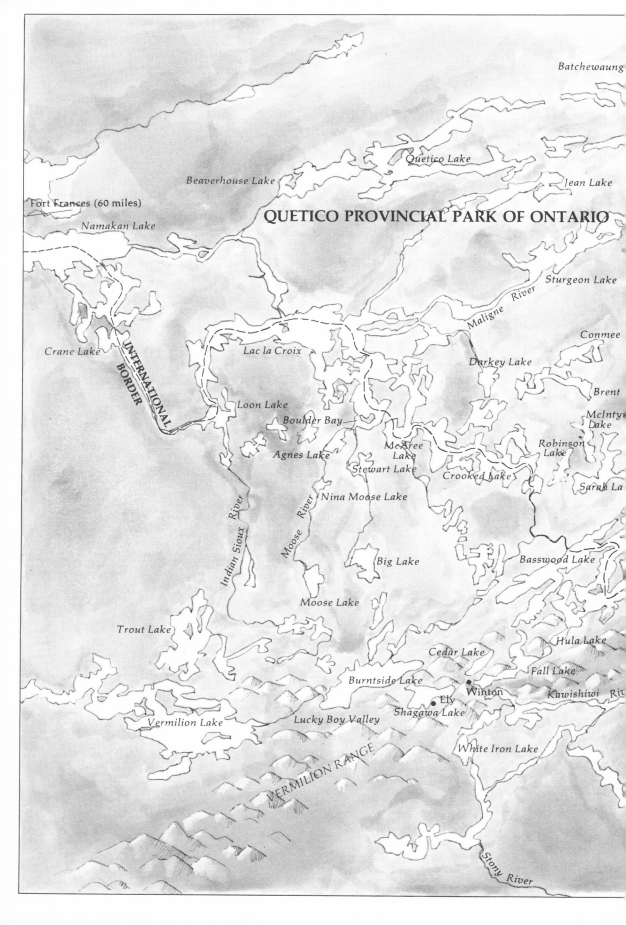

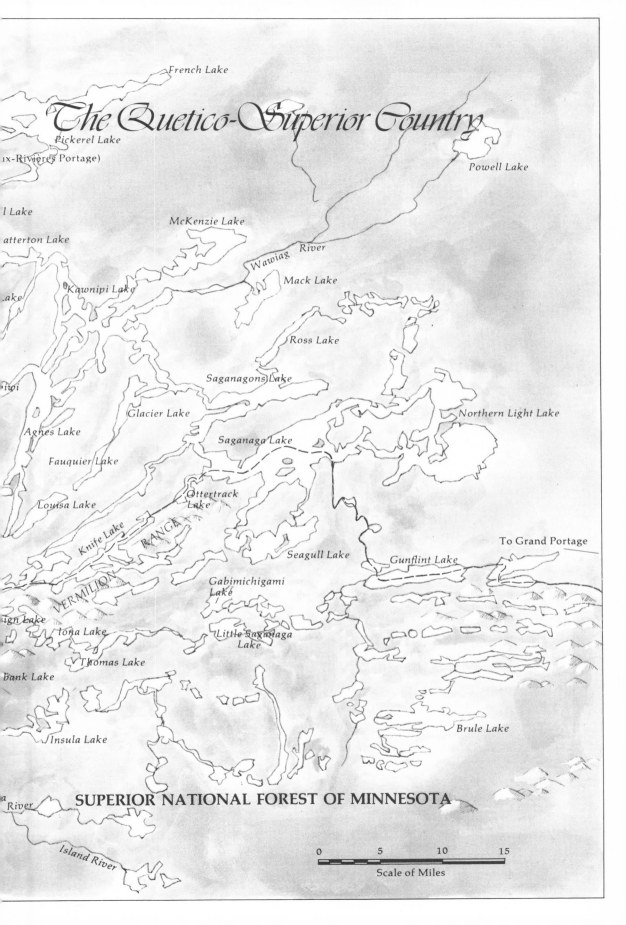

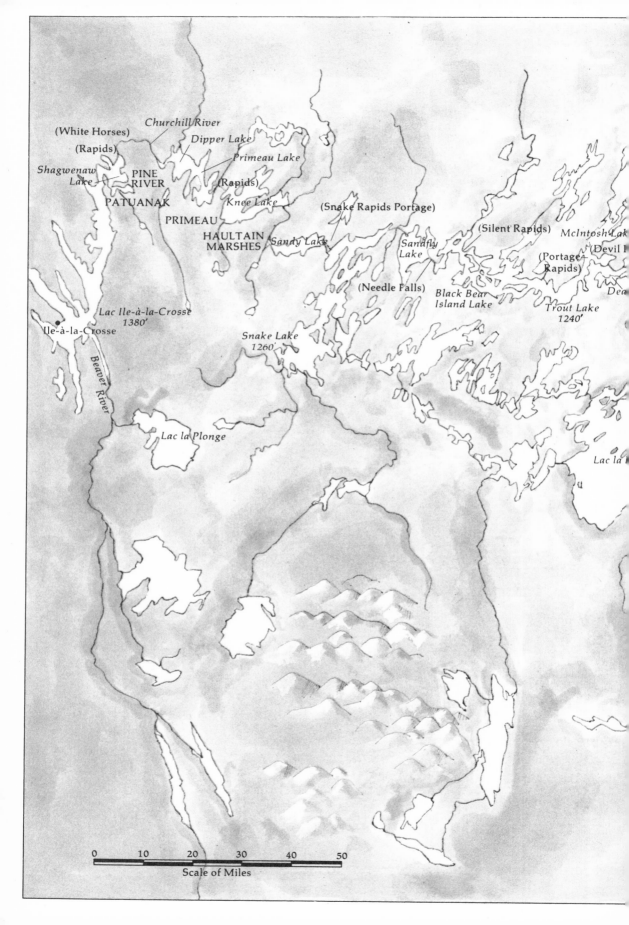

Western Churchill River Area

To Reindeer Lake

Reindeer River

Churchill River

Churchill River

SASKATCHEWAN

MANITOBA

apids)

ake

Mountain Lake

Stanley Mission

(Frog Portage)

(Keg Falls)

Keg Lake   Trade
Lake

Nistowiak Lake

(Grand Rapids)

Iskwatikan Lake

Manawan Lake

Wood Lake

(Rapids)

(Pelican Narrows)

Pelican Lake

Mirond Lake

Corneille
Lake

MALIGNE

Sturgeon Weir River

Flin Flon

Amisk
Lake

Goose Lake

Sturgeon Landing

Sturgeon Weir R.

Goose

River

Namew Lake

To the Pas

Cumberland Lake

Cumberland House

Saskatchewan River

Old Channel

A Note About the Author

Sigurd F. Olson was one of the country's well-known ecologists and interpretive naturalists with a sensitive, almost lyric response to nature. Throughout his books runs the thread of a deepening understanding and appreciation of the spiritual value of the wilderness—a heritage we are now in danger of destroying. He was recognized nationally with many awards and honorary degrees, and served as consultant to the federal government on wilderness preservation and ecological problems. President of the Wilderness Society, the National Parks Association, and adviser to the Izaak Walton League of America, his was a leading voice of environmental concern. Until his death in 1982, he observed life from the vantage point of his home in Ely, Minnesota, gateway to the Quetico-Superior region.

A Note About Design and Production

The text of this book was set by modern photocomposition. The text type is the film version of linotype Palatino, designed by Hermann Zapf. The display type is Vivaldi, designed by Friedrich Peter. It was composed, printed, and bound by Kingsport Press, Inc., Kingsport, Tennessee. The separations for the photographic inserts were prepared by Chanticleer Press in Italy and printed by Kingsport Press.

The book was designed by Lidia Ferrara with photographs by Dr. J. Arnold Bolz, illustrations by Francis Lee Jaques, Robert Hines, and Leslie Kouba, and maps by David Lindroth.